LIKE STARS FOR EVERMORE

Ana Méndez Ferrell

Voice Of The Light
MINISTRIES

LIKE STARS FOR EVERMORE

Publisher: Voice of The Light Ministries / United States of America
Category: Kingdom of God
Design / Edition: Ana Méndez Ferrell
Layout Design: Andrea Jaramillo

All rights reserved. This publication may not be reproduced or transmitted in any forms or any means, file in an electronic system nor transmitted in any electronic, mechanical way including photocopying, recording or by any information storage retrieval system, or in any other manner (including audiobooks), without previous written permission of the author.

All biblical references have been extracted from the New King James Version and in some cases translated from the Amplified Bible. We also use the Textual Bible.

Printed in the United States of America

www.voiceofthelight.com
1st English Edition 2021, Voice of The Light Ministries - P.O. Box 3418 Ponte Vedra, Florida, 32004 / U. S. A.

ISBN 978-1-944681-38-8

I thank my Heavenly Father, my beloved Lord Jesus, and His precious Holy Spirit for every revelation laid out in this book. To God alone be all the Glory.

I dedicate this book to all the children of Light that will shine like the stars forever and to this new generation arising, with the sole purpose of being a Light so that God may be known and glorified in the nations.

I also dedicate it to my grandchildren, Leon and Karem, whom I carry in my heart like a flaming torch of God's Love. They will carry the shinning and the banner to many generations.

FOREWORD

by Charlie Shamp

> Those who are wise shall shine like the brightness of the firmament, and those who turn many to righteousness like the stars forever and ever.
>
> | Daniel 12:3

In her groundbreaking work, Ana Méndez Ferrell pulls back the theological shades obscuring the bright lights of the heavenly realm and cluttering the landscape with religious rationalistic thinking. Most of the modern church has not been exposed to the supernatural world meant to be our home where our lives are transformed into Christ's likeness.

Like Stars For Evermore takes you down a road less traveled that was always there; we just did not see it. With eye-opening revelation, Ana reveals a truth that sets you free to be what you were always meant to be. Combining a theological perspective with prophetic insight, the light of her revelation brings life to ancient truths.

All Christians were exposed to the glorious truth of the resurrection but get ready because Ana will guide you to a place that will forever change your view of Christ's resurrection. Ana's viewpoint of the resurrection is more than a historical fact; it is a pathway to spiritual power and the entryway to the heritage belonging to every believer. Jesus' resurrection altered the chaos in Eden. His resurrection ushers you into the heavenly places where you reign with Christ in a renewed Eden, not only in the future but now.

This book opens your eyes to the Heavenly City's reality in our midst, and we learn to live and be changed in that heavenly place so you can manifest the Light of Christ. When you open her book, you will embark on an extraordinary voyage into God's Raqia, the ruling firmament in the heavens where the angelic hosts and the children of God gather together to rule with Christ Jesus.

There is an increasing interest in the apocryphal books, especially the book of Enoch. Some of the early church fathers created a bad rap to the book of Enoch and other apocryphal books, but not all. Some of the great church fathers embraced those books because of the spiritual value of their writings, including Clement of Alexandria, Tertullian, and Origen. But Ana does not dabble in these writings; she is a pioneer and gifted student of the ancient writings.

> From the wells of her prophetic experiences, she draws forth living waters that will quench your thirst for the heavenly realities. This is the day of the Lord when the light and the glory of Christ will shine brightly. For God, who said, "Light shall shine out of darkness," is the One who has shone in our hearts to give the Light of the knowledge of the glory of God in the face of Christ.
>
> | 2 Corinthians 4:6

This leads us to conclude that those who shine like the stars throughout perpetual eternity are on a spiritual quest to know God and His marvelous light. Ana's passion is illustrated on every page, a desire for seeing the sons and daughters of God led to be the purity, the love, and the righteousness of God that illuminates entire generations.

I highly recommend Ana Ferrell's new book, Like Stars For Evermore. It is the antidote for the hungry soul who longs to experience heaven's reality and desires to shine brightly in these dark days.

Charlie Shamp

Cofounder of Destiny Encounters International
Author, *Mystical Prayer and Transfigured*

INDEX

page 11	**Introduction**
page 15	**Chapter 1** The Books in Heaven
page 31	**Chapter 2** The Sons of Resurrection
page 61	**Chapter 3** Those Who Exist in Splendor
page 81	**Chapter 4** The Tabernacle of God with Men
page 103	**Chapter 5** How We Were Created Before the Foundation of the World
page 127	**Chapter 6** The Raqia
page 157	**Chapter 7** Connecting to Our Celestial Being

page 173 | **Chapter 8**
The Raqia's Government

page 185 | **Chapter 9**
Rest: The Key to Access
Heavenly Dimensions

page 199 | **Chapter 10**
What Manifests on the Earth
Depends on Us

page 205 | **Appendix 1**
History of the Canons

page 217 | **Appendix 2**
Lost Books Worth Considering

INTRODUCTION

We are living in a time of great change and revelation. I believe God put the world and church on pause this 2020 to reset the planet, our priorities, and our perceptions. God wants to restart new processes and draw our attention to the search of truths that have remained forgotten.

The events that have transpired never took place before, leading us to stop for a moment to understand better what God is speaking at this time.

Now is the hour for the wise, those with understanding, the children of Light, to be the instruments of great change upon the Earth.

Understanding the Light – who we are as eternal and celestial beings on Earth – is one of the main purposes for this writing.

We will dive into foundational subject matter such as the resurrection, but not in a historical sense of Christ's victory over death in His own body, but as an inheritance and the power that ushers us into the greatest of heavenly places.

This book will open your eyes to the Heavenly City's reality in our midst and how to live in it and through it.

We are going to embark on an extraordinary voyage into God's Raqia, the ruling firmament in the heavens where the angelic hosts and the children of God gather together to rule with Christ Jesus. This is a pioneering subject that God wants to shed His Light on so that His Will is done on Earth as it is in Heaven.

The first thing we will understand is from where the Bible was written. Because it's from that dimension that Scripture comes alive and the truths that the Writer sought to capture in it emerge. Also, this is how we can see things that we have never seen before.

This is a prophetic book written under an anointing of Light, sent from Heaven above to awaken the true children of the Most High. The Spirit of Prophecy manifests by activating in others an ever-deeper knowledge of Christ and His work.

Christ is the Spirit of prophecy, who prophesied Himself throughout the Old Testament and then came, in flesh, to establish heaven on the earth.

> Of this salvation the prophets have inquired and searched carefully, who prophesied of the grace that would come to you, searching what, or what manner of time, **the Spirit of Christ who was in them** was indicating when He testified beforehand the sufferings of Christ and the glories that would follow.
>
> | 1 Peter 1:10-11

The Spirit of Prophecy bears witness to Christ; it is given to bring us to the fullness of His knowledge. This is His essence, injecting every hearer with seeds of life that grow and develop within the one that receives them.

This is how we know that a prophecy came from God: by the seed sown that bears fruit in the one who hears and heeds it.

When the prophetic word leaves heaven, it illuminates pages from the Book of Life written in our spirit, and in some way, unveils the chapters that each of us has to live in God's times and seasons.

This is why this book is prophetic, because it is designed to awaken, in those with understanding, the Light that must shine within them.

We will enter the dimension in which we were created before the foundation of the world. We will know as we were known and receive the keys to reconnect ourselves with our true celestial being, like Adam when he was created. This is the inheritance that Jesus brought us by restoring Eden to us, here and now.

The wise aren't those who receive salvation, but those who understand how to radiate the Light of Christ to change the world they live in. Those who subdue this world's system so heaven can rule on earth. Those who not only teach righteousness but live it as well. These are the upright and pure at heart who can see God face to face.

> Those who are wise shall shine like the brightness of the firmament, and those who turn many to righteousness like the stars forever and ever.
>
> Many shall be purified, made white, and refined, but the wicked shall do wickedly; and none of the wicked shall understand, but the wise shall understand.
>
> **| Daniel 12:3, 10**

THE BOOKS IN HEAVEN

> And Enoch took up his parable, and said: There was a righteous man, whose eyes were opened by the Lord, and he saw a Holy vision in the heavens, which the angels showed to me, and I heard everything from them. And I understood what I saw, but not for this generation, **but for a distant generation that will come.**
>
> | Enoch 1:2

Since the time of Enoch, God has spoken to a future and distant generation. One that would shine and manifest the Light of Christ like no other. These are the wise and perfected ones spoken of by the prophet Daniel who would shine like the stars forever and ever.[1]

Enoch describes them as the humble, the mistreated, or as Jesus called them, the blessed who were persecuted for the truth, yet still loved their enemies as true Sons of God.

> For there are books, and records about them, in Heaven above, so that the angels may read them and know what is about to come upon the sinners. And upon the spirits of the humble, and of those who afflicted their bodies and were recompensed by God, and of those who were abused by evil men.
>
> And all their blessings I have recounted in the books, and He has assigned them their reward, for they were found to be such **that they loved Heaven more than their life in the world.** And even though they were trampled underfoot by evil men, and had to listen to reviling, and reproach from them, and were abused, yet they blessed their Lord.
>
> **| Enoch 108:7,10**

The author of the epistle to the Hebrews describes them as those of whom the world was not worthy, men and women of faith, who chose to die to this world, esteeming it as garbage, as Paul said.[2] They loved as Jesus loved, for their reward was not of this world.

[1] - Daniel 12:3

[2] - Hebrews 11:37-38

Enoch adds:

> And the Lord said: "And now I will summon the spirits of the good, who are of the Generation of Light, and I will transform those who were born in darkness, who in the flesh were not recompensed with honor as was fitting to their faith.
>
> **And I will bring out into the shining light those who love My Holy Name**, and I will set each one on the throne of his honor."
>
> And they will shine, for times without number, for righteous is the Judgement of God, for with the faithful He will keep faith in the dwelling of upright paths.
>
> And they will see those who were born in darkness, thrown into the darkness, **while the righteous shine.**
>
> And the sinners will cry out, as they see them shining, **but they themselves will go where days, and times, are prescribed for them.**
>
> **| Enoch 108:11-15**[3]

Why do I write about Enoch? Because I believe that he is one of the most powerful characters mentioned in the Bible, worthy of being studied by all those who love the truth of Christ and seek it above all things.

---

[3] - Translated from two English versions edited by Robert H. Charles and Hedley F. Sparks, and from the Francois Martin's French Version; last res which in turn were translated from Ethiopian manuscripts cross-checked with Greek manuscripts; and these versions corrected with Quran Aramean manuscripts. Edited by Jose T. Milik and translated into Spanish by Florentino García M.

Enoch has always elicited my absolute admiration. His walk with God was so intense and genuine that he was transferred not to see death. He simply walked with God, and one day without saying more, he disappeared into the heavens, changing dimensions without ever experiencing what the rest of humanity has to live through. He was a man who, before being translated, bore witness to having pleased God.

But how was it that he pleased God to such an extent that he lived immersed in heavenly places like no other man?

In his writings, we find an exchange between Lamech, his grandson, and Methuselah, whom he urges to speak to his grandfather Enoch, telling him:

> "And now, my father, I am here to petition thee and implore thee that thou mayest go to Enoch, our father, and learn from him the truth, **for his dwelling-place is amongst the angels**."
>
> **| Enoch 106:7**

Enoch lived in God's Kingdom dimensions, just as Jesus described them. A Kingdom that is not of this world where Heaven's reality is the realm that governs the Earth, the genuine habitation which Jesus prepared for the sons of Light. The place where we are eternally united to Jesus and from where we can take and manifest everything He has given us.

> In My Father's house are many mansions; if it were not so, I would have told you. I go to prepare a place for you.

> And if I go and prepare a place for you, I will come again and receive you to Myself; **that where I am, there you may be also.**
>
> And where I go you know, and the way you know."
>
> **| John 14:2-4**

Later, we will discover that this spiritual reality, manifested to Enoch, is the resurrection realm –the heavens joined to the Earth in Christ Jesus. It's the inheritance that He conquered for us. Moreover, it's also the depths to which the Apostle Paul refers to when he writes about the Kingdom of God, eternal life, the Heavenly Jerusalem, and the power of the resurrection.

Now, why was such a strong man left out of the Holy Scriptures? Isn't it important to know the Kingdom of Heaven as seen and understood by someone so unique in history?

It certainly is for me and for all those who long for their lives to shine by knowing God as no other generation before. These are those who serve and served this world as luminaries amid such dreadful darkness.

God is revealing Himself and entrusting things to those of us who love the truth and seek Him above everything else. His light is reserved for those who fear and seek Him early.

There are books and letters that, although extra-Biblical --in other words, outside of the official canon-- are pro-Biblical, and do not contradict it but shed a light to understand difficult portions of scripture.

These are known as Apocryphal books.[4] In this list, some manuscripts fully support all Biblical thinking, and others are, in essence, heretical.

1 | The Apocryphal and Historical Books

> Then I know another mystery: That books will be given to the righteous and wise, and will be a source of joy, and truth, and much wisdom. And books will be given to them, and they will believe in them, and rejoice over them; and all the righteous, who have learnt from them all the ways of truth, be recompensed.
>
> **| Enoch 104:12-13**

Although this book is not about those writings, I will be mentioning some passages that are analogous to the Holy Scriptures. Not to impose anything, nor for them to be treated as God's infallible word, but only as authors who said things that were very relevant in their time.

For this, I want to share a little background to expand your knowledge concerning some of these books and why I deem it fair to unearth them.

The big question that came up in my heart was, could there be hidden treasures in writings strategically preserved by God or diabolically snatched? Has all that God is and left written down been given to us? Or have there been instruments throughout history that have tried to deny us such precious documents? Religious and rational men who simply did not understand them. Could it be that

---

[4] Appendix 1 at the end of the book

some ancient scrolls and letters never made it to Rome when the Catholic Canon was decided but were part of the Orthodox or Coptic canon?

After writing fifteen books –fourteen of them published– I realized that it was impossible for apostles the likes of Peter, to have only written two letters, or John only one gospel, the book of Revelation, and three epistles. And what about Nathanael to whom Jesus said, "And He said to him, 'Most assuredly, I say to you, hereafter you shall see heaven open, and the angels of God ascending and descending upon the Son of Man.'[5]

Did this beloved disciple ever write anything? And what about the other Apostles?

John wrote:

> And there are also many other things that Jesus did, which if they were written one by one, I suppose that even the world itself could not contain the books that would be written. Amen.
>
> **| John 21:25**

These questions moved my spirit to research the truth of how the Bible was really put together.

After much searching, I have discovered that many documents were seized by the Vatican, the London Museum, and Egypt. Many others were held captive in Alexandria, and still, others were hidden in caves such as Qumran or Nag Hammadi[6] to keep them from being

---

[5] - John 1:51

[6] - In 1945, some Egyptian farmers were digging in the desert for fertilizer nitrates about 10 kilometers from the modern city of Nag Hammadi. They unearthed a large clay jug containing 12

destroyed by their persecutors. Others are yet to be discovered.

In Appendixes 1 and 2, I lay out a brief history of how the canons were formed in the different early churches as well as today's Bible canon. I also provide a short historical description of the apocryphal books that I consider essential. The latter is for those who wish to know more about this subject and lay a foundation for knowing certain books.

To dive into the territory of these forgotten manuscripts, we need four basic items:

1• To have an in-depth knowledge of God.

2• To be searchers and understanders of the Holy Scriptures.

3• To know the church's history from its beginning, its protagonists, and the sources of opposition they faced.

4• To know how to listen and be led by the Holy Spirit.

Without these four foundations, it is extremely risky to try to discern and study the apocryphal books.[7]

None of these four items work isolated from the rest, and we must not ignore any if we yearn to find the truth.

---

leather-bound papyrus codexes on covered in leather, and part of a thirteenth, all written in Coptic. These fourth-century books containing forty-six different treaties of varying length, most of them previously unknown, make up what is now known as the Nag Hammadi Library. The majority are «Gnostic» writings considered heretical by the ancient fathers of the church. The second treaty of Codex II of Nag Hammadi consists of a complete collection of 114 sayings attributed to Jesus, with the title «The Gospel according to Thomas». The publication of this Gospel in 1959 made it possible for scholars to demonstrate that the Oxyrhnchus papyri came from three different Greek copies of the Gospel of Thomas, the full text of which is now preserved only in the form of the Coptic translation belonging to the Nag Hammadi Collection

[7] - Appendix 1 at the end of book

He, who does not have all four, has none at all. He who despises any of them despises all four. Error after error has been made due to their separation, becoming wise in their own understanding. The same aberrations happen to those who base their knowledge on spiritual fantasies full of dreams and visions without God's knowledge and scriptural foundation.

The truth is gradually revealed from within our spirit when we live lives of integrity, in the fear of God, making His knowledge the essence of who we are and what we say.

Knowing Him is to live what He is, in and through us. And it is in the light of this understanding, guided by His Wisdom, that we can go deeper into discerning what is true and what is false.

> **Those who are wise** shall shine like the brightness of the firmament; and those who turn many to righteousness like the stars forever and ever.
>
> **| Daniel 12:3**

One of the problems we face are the legacies left behind by Bishops Irenaeus and Athanasius in the early centuries.[8] They have been why the Christian church has rejected the "Books and Letters of the Apocrypha" as contrary to the Bible. And in fact, some are but not all.

Some of these were part of books and letters studied by the Early Church, such as the Book of Jasher mentioned in Joshua 10:13 and 2 Samuel 1:18, the Books of Enoch and Thomas, the Gospel of Truth by Valentinus, and

---

[8] - II and IV Centuries respectively.

others that were part of the Coptic Church canons and the Eastern churches such as Siria.

In his book, Lost Christianities, Bart D. Ehrman writes:

> "The Early Church did not consist of a single orthodoxy from which various heretical minorities later departed"…" on the contrary"…" Christianity took on a significant variety of forms in antiquity, none of which clearly represented a substantial majority of believers at the expense of the rest.[9]

The other great dilemma is that very few people study history and search within it for great knowledge sources. It enlightens us, for example, by showing us how relevant the Book of Enoch was at the beginning of the church. Respectable scholars and theologians of the Word of God assure us that Enoch left a record. It is said that this book was initially written in Hebrew and Aramaic and that the first-century church studied it and had a great appreciation for it, as witnessed in the canonical epistles of Jude (6 and 14-16) and Peter (2:4). Some apocryphal letters[10] testify to the use of these books by the church of that time.

The Book of Enoch is also one of the most studied books by Jewish scholars and theologians and has aroused great interest among the Prophetic Church and the New Reformation of the Spirit.

The words that God has spoken through His prophets, and those yet to be said, remain alive in the heavens, ensuring

---

[9] - Bart D. Ehrman, Lost Christianities, pg's. 254 and 259. Crítica Ed., 2009

[10] - The writings of Justin Martir (100-165 AD); Athenagoras (170 AD); Tatian (110-172 AD); Irenaeus, Bishop of Lyon (115-185); Clement of Alexandria (150-220); Tertullian (160-230); Lactantius (260-325) and others.

they will be made manifest.

Everything that God has spoken generation after generation is recorded in the heavenly books, whether we have them in the catholic canon[11] or not.

> Forever, O Lord, **Your word is settled in heaven**. Your faithfulness endures to all generations; You established the earth, and it abides. They continue this day according to Your ordinances, **for all are Your servants**.
>
> | Psalms 119:89-91

> The grass withers, the flower fades, but the word of our God stands forever."
>
> | Isaiah 40:8

Many of the Old Testament prophets did not write for their time but for generations to come.

King David said:

> Now also when I am old and grayheaded, O God, do not forsake me, until I declare Your strength to this generation, **Your power to everyone who is to come.**
>
> | Psalms 71:18

Enoch spoke of books written in heaven, reading in some of them of the great judgment by flood with which God destroyed all creation.

---

[11] - The canon was constituted by the Catholic Church in the IV Century.

> For there are books, and records about them, in Heaven above, so that the Angels may read them and know what is about to come upon the sinners...
>
> | Enoch 108[12]

> For I know the mysteries of the Holy Ones, for the Lord showed them to me, and made them known to me, and I read them in the Tablets of Heaven.
>
> | Enoch 106

The Bible supports these passages when it speaks about the books being opened in Revelation or when it mentions the Lamb's book of life. Zachariah saw in visions a scroll that was flying. Both Ezekiel and John were given a heavenly scroll and a[13] little book to eat, respectively, which were sweet to the mouth and bitter in the stomach.

Ezekiel also received a heavenly scroll of lamentations.[14]

> Now when I looked, there was a hand stretched out to me; and behold, a scroll of a book was in it.
>
> Then He spread it before me; and there was writing on the inside and on the outside and written on it were lamentations and mourning and woe.
>
> | Ezekiel 2:9-10

[12] Book of Enoch, Scribd library https://www.scribd.com/read/356959231/The-Complete-Book-of-Enoch-Standard-English-Version#b_search-menu_446751

[13] In Appendix 2, You can find the origin and description

[14] -Revelation 13:8, 20:12 / Zechariah 5:1 / Ezekiel 3:2

There are many things recorded throughout history in the books of the Jewish people's oral traditions, which we do not see directly in the Bible. However, they are not opposed to it, but they shed light on extraordinary events around it. An example is that the Law was revealed to the Patriarch Abraham before Moses, and he passed it on to his generations. We cannot know how this happened with the Bible alone, but if I extend my understanding by delving into historical books, I will find the light I need.

> Because Abraham obeyed My voice and kept My charge, My commandments, My statutes, and My laws.
>
> **| Genesis 26:5**

Another example of things that we have no idea how they happened just by reading Moses' Genesis is that there was a divine priesthood before Aaron:

> Then Melchizedek king of Salem brought out bread and wine; he was the **priest of God Most High.** And he blessed him and said: "Blessed be Abram of God Most High, Possessor of heaven and earth.
>
> **| Genesis 14:18**

This Melchizedek left a book of much value called "The Great Melchizedek Scroll."

Another mystery is, why Noah was considered a righteous man? Based on what law? And how did God choose him?

> This is the genealogy of Noah. Noah was a just man, perfect in his generations. **Noah walked with God.**
>
> | **Genesis 6:9**

But by reading the Book of Enoch, I will find an excellent account of who Noah was, his wisdom, and how he was chosen from his mother's womb.

All this to say that a new page is opening in the heavenly books. In Jesus, we have received the abundant treasures of His Glory and Wisdom. We have been granted the power to access the heavens and all their dimensions. The heavens and the Earth are one in Jesus, and a generation of Light will read the books in heaven designed for this time.

> Now, therefore, I swear to you, the righteous, by the glory of the Great and Honored and Mighty One in dominion, and by His greatness I swear to you.
>
> I know a mystery
> And have read the heavenly tablets,
> And have seen the holy books,
> And have found written therein and inscribed regarding them
>
> | **Enoch 103**

The Book of Enoch, which I will reference in various parts of this writing, has emerged with great interest and is being studied by serious men and women of God of our time.

While the Bible is the anchor of our faith and nothing can ever take its place, there are, however, certain Apocryphal and historical writings that, as I said earlier, enlighten us to understand passages that can be complex and difficult to interpret.

Thus, this is what interests me. To bring light to the scriptures and support everything that I write with the most rigorous Biblical underpinning. On the other hand, I'm also a strong advocate of historical and cultural knowledge to better understand things written thousands of years ago. Research and scrutiny of all things are a sign of a thriving spirit in Christ.

The Apostle Paul wrote:

> However, we speak wisdom among those who are mature, yet not the wisdom of this age, nor of the rulers of this age, who are coming to nothing.
>
> But we speak the wisdom of God in a mystery, the hidden wisdom which God [a]ordained before the ages for our glory,
>
> which none of the rulers of this age knew; for had they known, they would not have crucified the Lord of glory.
>
> But as it is written:
> *"Eye has not seen, nor ear heard,*
> *Nor have entered into the heart of man*
> *The things which God has prepared for those who love Him."*

> *But God has revealed them to us through His Spirit.* ***For the Spirit searches all things, yes, the deep things of God.***

| 1 Corinthians 2:6-10

One of the most interesting verses concerning this thirst, which the Spirit gives to search the deep things of God, was written by Thomas the apostle in his gospel.

> And he said: He who shall find the interpretation of these sayings shall not taste of death.
>
> Jesus said: He who seeks, let him not cease seeking until he finds; and when he finds he will be troubled, and if he is troubled, he will be amazed, and he will reign over the All.

| Gospel of Thomas 1-2 - Apocryphal

All of this leads us to conclude that the "wise men and women" who shine like the stars throughout perpetual eternity are those on a spiritual quest, who know God and His marvelous light. They are Sons and daughters of God led to be the purity, the love, and the righteousness of God that illuminate entire generations.

It's not my intention to impose anything on anyone, but to illustrate principles that must be understood at this time; entirely Biblical foundations that need to be intensely scrutinized and read with a genuine spiritual understanding. The passages that I will mention, taken from the Apocryphal books, serve only as support and not a doctrine's foundation.

Chapter 2

SONS OF THE RESURRECTION

1 | What is the Resurrection?

To speak of the eternal light, of those who shine forever and ever, leads us to study how the resurrection is the fundamental power for this to happen.

The resurrection is connected to faith and righteousness. Both are part of God's invisible kingdom and form the necessary substance for the divine to manifest itself on the Earth.

The resurrection is the foundation of our faith. It's not just a historical event, but it's the power Jesus came to bring to the Earth.

A vast majority of people have an idea of the resurrection as a moment in a distant future when suddenly the graves will open, and the dead will come out and fill the Earth. However, this is a concept we have dragged from the Catholic Church, void of any foundation in the Old and New Testaments.

We need to understand that everything Jesus spoke was to confirm what was already prophesied in the Old Testament, since it's the type and the shadow of all that is true, which is Himself.

So, when we seek the resurrection concept in the Old Covenant, we find very few scripture references. The first is found in the book of the Prophet Hosea.

> After two days He will revive us; on the third day He will raise us up, that we may live in His sight.

| Hosea 6:2

Here, the Spirit of God shows us a different view of the historical fact of Christ's resurrection and the fable of the resurrection portrayed in renaissance paintings. This is Christ's glorious resurrection work. The resurrection is His design for us all. For some, it will be after death, but for the wise (those with understanding), it can be while we are still alive.

Now let us see how Jesus, who is the resurrection, speaks about this subject:

> "Most assuredly, I say to you, he who hears My word and believes in Him who sent Me

> has everlasting life, and shall not come into judgment, but has passed from death into life.
>
> Most assuredly, I say to you, the hour is coming, and now is, when the dead will hear the voice of the Son of God; and those who hear will live.
>
> For as the Father has life in Himself, so He has granted the Son to have life in Himself,.
>
> **| John 5:24-26**

The hour is coming, and now is! All that Jesus came to do is designed for a clear manifestation in the present or the now since He is the great "I Am."

Jesus, who is the resurrection, was going to speak to every spirit in a state of death –the condition of man's spirit before receiving the life of Christ.

Resurrection has to do with the type of life that dwells in us, the seventh day of creation, the rest from all of our works, and the Kingdom of God.

Paul exhorts us by saying:

> Therefore, if you died with Christ from the basic principles of the world…
>
> **If then you were raised with Chris**t, seek those things which are above, where Christ is, sitting at the right hand of God.
>
> **| Colossians 2:20 & 3:1**

Paul is talking about dying to this world's system, its rudiments, and the control it has over our lives. When we die to the ruling of our own soul and yield to the Lordship of Christ, our spirit enters a state of resurrection.

We must die to Adam's fallen nature to enter into the nature of Jesus Christ. The problem is that within the all-inclusive, look warm church of this century, most people tend to avoid this fundamental principle.

When Jesus Christ rose from the dead, He not only manifested God's magnificent power in conquering death and hell, but He also took us along with Him to live by the resurrection. This is the divine power that makes us sons and heirs of God: Christ being the resurrection and us raised together with Him.

The resurrection is the atmosphere and the power of the spiritual realm of the Kingdom. It was the Glory of God that descended into the deepest parts of the Earth and raised Christ from the dead. Thus, to understand the resurrection is to know who we are and the power that we have.

Paul understood this was the source of power of the Gospel and the way to successfully bring about the work of Jesus Christ.

He also prayed that we would be filled with the knowledge of God, His wisdom and revelation so the eyes of our understanding would be enlightened, to know our inheritance, which are all the riches of God's Glory.

Concerning this, he says:

> And what is the exceeding greatness of His

> power toward us who believe, according to the working of His mighty power, **which He worked in Christ when He raised Him from the dead** and seated Him at His right hand in the heavenly places.
>
> | Ephesians 1:19-20

He stresses here that the resurrection is not just a historical fact but the true power and heritage of every believer. This is the reason why Paul is going to pursue the resurrection in all its design, setting his eyes on the absolute knowledge of God, even if it means having to give up everything else in this life.

> Yet indeed I also count all things loss for the excellence of the knowledge of Christ Jesus my Lord, for whom I have suffered the loss of all things, and count them as rubbish, that I may gain Christ and be found in Him, not having my own righteousness, which is from the law, but that which is through faith in Christ, the righteousness which is from God by faith;
>
> **that I may know Him and the power of His resurrection**, and the fellowship of His sufferings, being conformed to His death, if, by any means, I may attain to the resurrection from the dead.
>
> **Not that I have already attained,** or am already perfected; but I press on, that I may lay hold of that for which Christ Jesus has also laid hold of me.
>
> | Philippians 3:8-12

I want you to notice something quite powerful here: Paul says that it is through faith that we can know Him and the power of the resurrection.

So, in this statement, faith is not aimed at getting a house or a car, but it seeks to receive God's knowledge and this particular glory that comes by the resurrection.

Now, Paul also says something that draws my attention...

if, by any means, I may attain to the resurrection from the dead. We must open our understanding here. He is talking about something that stretches far beyond the generic resurrection that everyone experiences after death – some unto eternal life and others unto eternal damnation.

Paul was absolutely sure that, at some point after death, he would rise again. His entire theology and everything he heard from the Father is that the just shall be raised in Christ Jesus. By saying, *if by any means I may attain to the resurrection from the dead,* Paul can't be referring to something in the future, but to a resurrection he wishes to attain in life. He is seeking to know God the way he must be known –through the power of the resurrection. That is why he emphasizes, *not that I have already attained it.* He is pursuing something that one can or can't achieve and that he seeks by all means to attain.

I want to show you how Paul certainly believed that the resurrection was something that could be attained in life.

For this, we need to remove any preconceived ideas of how we imagined the resurrection of the dead to be and see how Jesus really spoke about this subject.

2 | The Resurrection isn't a Future Concept, but a Present One

A. | How did Jesus speak about the Resurrection?

The disciples asked Jesus a question about the resurrection, giving an example of seven brothers who, as each one died, went on marrying the same woman.

> Therefore, in the resurrection, whose wife does she become? For all seven had her as wife."
>
> Jesus answered and said to them, "**The sons of this age** marry and are given in marriage. But those who are **counted worthy to attain that age**, and the resurrection from the dead, neither marry nor are given in marriage; nor can they die anymore, for they are equal to the angels and are sons of God, **being sons of the resurrection.**
>
> | Luke 20:33-36

The Lord is speaking of two different dimensions here. One is "the sons of this age" or those under this world's system, and the other are "those who attain the age to come", that is, the Kingdom of God.

When he refers to "this age," it has to do with the earthly things, the temporal, and man's fallen nature.

On the other hand, when we hear the words "coming age" or "in that age," our natural mind immediately shifts to the future. But the "coming age" refers to the one that began when heaven and Earth were once again joined together in Christ Jesus. Before Christ, these were separate, but after His resurrection, they were unified as in the beginning.

> Having made known to us the mystery of His will, according to His good pleasure which He purposed in Himself,
>
> that in the dispensation of the fullness of the times He might gather together in one all things in Christ, both which are in heaven and which are on earth—in Him.
>
> **| Ephesians 1:9-10**

Now let's see when this dispensation of the fullness of the times takes place.

> But Christ came as High Priest of the **good things to come**, with the greater and more perfect tabernacle not made with hands, that is, not of this creation.
>
> **| Hebrews 9:11**

Here we see that Jesus takes the priesthood of that "age to come," or the so-called "good things to come," that "era" that was beginning, which had nothing to do with the earthly one.

The author of the book of Hebrews clearly establishes that the fullness of the times is determined by the sacrifice on the Cross, with a new time or era beginning as of that moment –This is called: the Messianic Era or the Era of the Kingdom of God.

> He then would have had to suffer often since the foundation of the world; **but now, once at the end of the ages**, He has appeared to put away sin by the sacrifice of Himself.
>
> | Hebrews 9:26

This is what Jesus is talking about to His disciples concerning the resurrection. He wanted them to understand that this coming age is the spiritual realm where the heavens and the earth have once again come together.

You see there are two ways to live in this world: one is according to this world's system, and the other is in the dimensions of the Kingdom of God, which is the realm of the resurrection.

Now, when Jesus says that those who are counted worthy to attain that age do not marry nor are given in marriage, He is by no means saying that married people cannot enter the Kingdom of God. Because if that were the case, Peter would not have been able to enter either since he was a married man. We know this because Jesus healed his mother-in-law.

It is also very likely that Paul was also married since no one could have been a part of the Sanhedrin[15] in that day in time, unless they were married. He was likely widowed.

What Jesus is emphasizing here is that our cares and desires, what people want to achieve in this world, are different from what one aspires in God's Kingdom.

---

[15] - The Sanhedrin, was in fact, the Supreme Court of Jewish Law, whose mission was to administrate justice by interpreting and applying the Torah, the sacred law. It was made up of the elders of Israel. Some of them even married the Torah.

In this world's system, marriage is part of a design for human beings' multiplication during our time in the flesh. However, in that example, Jesus wanted to lead them to an understanding that would stretch them beyond the natural realm.

Jesus came as the latter Adam to restore Eden and to reunite Heaven and Earth that were separated by sin. He came to bring us the heavenly city and the realm where everything is possible. Indeed, He came to make all things new.

God wants to raise a remnant of Sons of the resurrection on the Earth. Those who become worthy because they loved Heaven more than the Earth. Who set their treasures above and pass-through this world as pilgrims and strangers. Those who sought to know God above everything else for HE is the greatest wealth they can ever cherish.

I believe that God is speaking these things because it's possible for some of us to one day become like Enoch, who was transferred to Heaven without ever tasting death. Men and women who walk with God and are one day simply snatched to another dimension and just remain there.

Thus, we see that being a son of God is very different from today's the concept, in which you can practically be a Christian any which way you want.

Even Paul Himself hoped for this glory of the resurrection that must manifest in the children of God, so that they could put an end to the bondage of creation.

> For I consider that the sufferings of this present time are not worthy to be compared with the glory which shall be revealed in us. For the earnest expectation of the creation eagerly waits for the revealing of the sons of God.
>
> **| Romans 8:18-19**

3 | To God, The Dead In Him Are Alive

Now let's go back to the passage in Luke 20, where Jesus continues to explain how the resurrection isn't a futuristic concept but a present one.

> But even Moses showed in the burning bush passage that the dead are raised, when he called the Lord 'the God of Abraham, the God of Isaac, and the God of Jacob.' For He is not the God of the dead but of the living, for all live to Him.
>
> **| Luke 20:37-38**

From the divine perspective, we see that everyone who is a son of God is not dead but resurrected.

Jesus was not talking to them about a resurrection after death in which some will have eternal life, and others will be condemned, but He's talking about those who were counted as worthy and have attained "that age". It's the dimension where Jesus Christ is the High Priest of all the good things to come, of every heavenly gift. He's talking about those who can live Eden on Earth while they are still in this world.

These are the sons of God, ambassadors of Heaven, whose spirit emanates the glory that dispels all darkness. Those who know God, who dwell in the resurrection and make the earth alive in their wake; But for this to happen, I need to change my understanding and believe that the resurrection is achievable in life. Once this happens and I begin to believe it with all my strength, something starts to happen even within my own cells.

This is the life of the Most High God, the eternal life that consumes everything mortal and embodies within us, bringing life to all our surroundings.

Entering into His rest is the realm of the resurrection and the realm of continuous movement, of rest in motion.

In the Apocryphal Gospel of Thomas, Jesus says something in line with what is described in the book of Luke.

> Jesus said: If they say to you: Where did you come from? tell them: We have come from the light, the place where the light came into being by itself and established itself and became visible through their image.[16]
>
> If they say to you: Who are you? say: We are his sons, and we are the chosen of the Living Father. If they ask you: What is the sign of your Father in you? tell them: It is a movement within restfulness.

---

[16] - The images mentioned here represent our being before the world was. He knew us and gave us a name to create us on Earth (Ephesians 1).

> His disciples said to him: On what day will the rest of the dead come into being? And on what day will the new world come? He said to them: That which ye await has come, but ye know it not.
>
> | **Thomas 50 & 51**

"That age" is the realm where time does not exist. It's the place where God dwells, the seventh day of creation, the Kingdom of God, where everything that you were before the foundation of the world has already been activated. It is the same Light that stretched out over the primeval chaos, existing within it, all that would ever be created, forever and ever.

In the realm of the resurrection, we are like the angels. And these are not looking at how to marry, how to do business, or how to procreate. But in this state, we can come and go from the heavenly dimensions where functions and assignments are quite different from the earthly ones.

Of course, we can be married in this state, have children, or own a business. But our priorities must always remain in Heaven above.

4 | A Glorified Body

Now, when Jesus resurrected, many rose with Him.

> And Jesus cried out again with a loud voice and yielded up His spirit.

> Then, behold, the veil of the temple was torn in two from top to bottom; and the earth quaked, and the rocks were split, and the graves were opened; and many bodies of the saints who had fallen asleep were raised; and coming out of the graves after His resurrection, they went into the holy city and appeared to many.
>
> **| Matthew 20:50-53**

The strange thing here is that no scripture explains how these resurrected people interacted with the Early Church. This happening was absolutely outstanding, unusual. They might have seen King David, Abraham, Moses, yet there isn't a single testimony of anyone having spoken or shared with them. Nor were they present on the Day of Pentecost in the upper room. There is a reason for this, and we will understand it as we look carefully on the resurrection of Jesus Christ.

When He rose from the dead, He didn't even need to remove the stone. The stone was removed either by the resurrection's impact or by the two angels that guarded the tomb. It was for a testimony to the Romans and to all those who were to believe. In His resurrected body, Jesus could pass through walls; He did not need to remove the stone Himself to leave the tomb.

In His resurrected body, He was continuously changing His appearance. Every time Jesus appeared to His disciples, He did so with a different countenance, so they could not recognize Him. The two disciples on the road to Emmaus thought He was a stranger. When Jesus appeared in the midst of the eleven, His countenance was already different.

They believed He was a spirit and were frightened. Peter and the other disciple did not identify Him as the one who had been walking with them just moments before in the road to Emmaus.

Mary thought He was the gardener. She didn't realize who he was until He called her by name.

The same thing happens the third time Jesus appeared to them..

> After these things Jesus showed Himself again to the disciples at the Sea of Tiberias, and in this way, He showed Himself:
>
> But when the morning had now come, Jesus stood on the shore; yet the disciples did not know that it was Jesus.
>
> **| John 21:1 & 4**

Now, why did He continually change His countenance? Because our glorified body has nothing to do with our natural face.

It's also interesting to note that during the time between the resurrection and the ascension, Jesus never slept on Earth.

Jesus no longer needed to live or abide according to the needs and customs required in a physical body. He was the high priest of the coming era and had already united the heavens and the Earth in Himself. As a resurrected being, He could come and go from Heaven to Earth as many times as He pleased.

If I were to analyze what a resurrected body is like, Jesus is the prototype and design that leads me into all truth of what it means to be in that state.

So, if I were to follow the same model, the same way that Christ interacted with His disciples after the resurrection, it is possible that the saints who came out of their tombs only showed themselves as a testimony and then ascended once again into the heavenly places. There is also the possibility that they appeared with a different countenance and continued to appear when someone needed something, acting as angels when they take human form to help us and then disappear.

Isn't this exactly what Jesus said? *Those that were counted as worthy shall be like the angels and are sons of God, being the sons of the resurrection.*[17]

Some things are hard to believe because we are structured by what we are in this world. However, we are entering a season when there will be some that believe it and see it.

When the Apostle Paul hears this word, about some counted as worthy to attain the resurrection, he pours Himself entirely into this promise, for he had begotten a pearl that he needed to find at all costs.

Paul knew that God had already predestined him for this resurrection in life. But he also understood that he needed to unify with his heavenly design for it to become a reality on Earth. Above all else, he longed to be counted worthy, but he knew that it required him to see things in a very different way than one does in the natural.

[17] - Luke 20:36

5 | The Upward Call Of God

Let's look again at the passage in Philippians, where Paul considers everything as garbage. Such is the glory he sees in the resurrection that assigning value to any vain thing here on earth would become the greatest obstacle to reaching his goal.

> ...for whom I have suffered the loss of all things, and count them as rubbish, that I may gain Christ...
>
> **...that I may know Him and the power of His resurrection**, and the fellowship of His sufferings, being conformed to His death, **if, by any means, I may attain to the resurrection from the dead.**
>
> **Not that I have already attained,** or am already perfected; but I press on, that I may lay hold of that for which Christ Jesus has also laid hold of me.
>
> **| Philippians 3:8b, 11-12a**

By expressing the words, if by any means I may attain to the resurrection from the dead, it is clear that he searches for Jesus not as a model of life, but in the dimension of the risen Christ.

He then adds, not that I have already attained it, obviously not referring to the latter resurrection which does not depend on us, nor on our worthiness, but on Christ. He goes on saying:

> Brethren, I do not count myself to have apprehended; but one thing I do, forgetting those things which are behind
>
> and reaching forward to those things which are ahead, I press toward the goal for the prize of the upward call of God in Christ Jesus.

| Philippians 3:12-15

Paul, who never knew Jesus in the flesh, was taught directly by Him in the spirit.[18] Not only did he hear all of His teachings first-hand, but He was also taken up into the third heaven where he heard unspeakable words.[19]

I believe that it was in this experience in heaven and paradise that he saw himself being laid hold of by Jesus and receiving the impartation of the resurrection of Christ. And not only did he see himself, but also all those that were to be counted worthy as well. This was the race he was determined to run, the upward call, which meant conquering this great goal: the resurrection in life. What he had seen and experienced in these heavenly dimensions, now had to become palpable and visible in his human nature.

This was the valued possession of his inheritance, which was rooted in the City of God. He had already received his citizenship in the Heavens, and now, to bring these riches and power down to earth he needed to pass through this world not lured by anything on it.

[18] Galatians 1:11-12

[19] 2 Corinthians 12:1-4

So, he closes his instruction to the Philippians by saying:

> For our citizenship is in heaven, from which we also eagerly wait for the Savior, the Lord Jesus Christ, who will transform our lowly body that it may be conformed to His glorious body, according to the working by which He is able even to subdue all things to Himself.
>
> **| Philippians 3:20-21**

This citizenship and this belonging to heavenly places actually grant us the possibility to be transformed into the body of the Glory of Jesus. So, he closes his instruction to the Philippians by saying:

If then you were raised with Christ, seek those things which are above, where Christ is, sitting at the right hand of God[20], that is, the heavenly city where God has given us a place therein.

This search became Paul's lifelong obsession and driving force, which he expresses in different ways throughout his epistles. It was the same search that constituted Abraham as the father of the faith.

> By faith he dwelt in the land of promise as in a foreign country, dwelling in tents with Isaac and Jacob, the heirs with him of the same promise; **for he waited for the city which has foundations, whose builder and maker is God.**
>
> **| Hebrews 11:9-10**

---

[20] Colosians 3:1

The perfection of God's children is found in being children of the resurrection. Not only to live by this power and this foundation, but also to resurrect everything around us. First, the dead in spirit who do not know the Lord, and those who die in the natural. It is the power to resurrect all that has been invaded by death, such as health, relationships, entire congregations, businesses, careers, ministries, and even nations whose design is to be filled with the life of God.

Now let's see how Paul expresses this same thought to the saints at Corinth and how the heavenly city is intimately linked to the power of the resurrection.

6 | The Heavenly City And Our Eternal Habitation

> For we know that if our earthly house, this tent, is destroyed, we have a building from God, a house not made with hands, eternal in the heavens.
>
> For in this we groan, earnestly desiring to be clothed with our habitation which is from heaven,
>
> | 2 Corinthians 5:1-2

Once again, by reading this in our natural reasoning, it would seem to refer to something after our demise. Yet, Paul isn't emphasizing life after death, nor the eternal mansions, but the heavenly dwelling place that must clothe us in life.

> If indeed, **having been clothed, we shall not be found naked.** For we who are in this tent groan, being burdened,
>
> not because we want to be unclothed, but further clothed, that mortality may be swallowed up by life.
>
> **| 2 Corinthians 5:3-4**

Here, he is not talking about the garments of grace and salvation. We do not need to groan for these, which are freely given to us by faith. But he is emphasizing that which determines whether we enter eternal life clothed or naked. The apostle himself says that he groans anxiously to be clothed with this heavenly habitation so that everything belonging to death is swallowed up by life.

What else can this garment be if not the power of the resurrection? These are the garments of the heavenly city, wherein the body of our humiliation transforms into the body of His Glory.

He anxiously groans because he believes wholeheartedly that his glorious transformation can be given to him while still alive. That is why he writes: that all mortality may be swallowed up by life, which implies that the resurrection life, which is Christ, can absorb in life our earthly and mortal nature, and clothing us in Glory.

He goes on to speak to the Corinthians, in this same epistle, on how to reach this transformation.

> But we all, with unveiled face, beholding as in a mirror the glory of the Lord, are being

> **transformed into the same image from glory to glory**, just as by the Spirit of the Lord.
>
> | 2 Corinthians 3:18

That is what Paul saw when he was taken up into paradise and the third heaven, where he entered into the Heavenly City and saw how our bodies were transformed. The more we take the time to enter into His rest, to connect with His glory dimension and with the city of the living God, the more we are transformed from glory to glory.

I believe that if Paul hadn't been beheaded, he might have very well been transposed like Enoch. Perhaps, he considered it more glorious to be sacrificed than to be transposed when he was sentenced.

Let's look at another portion of scripture where Paul continues to expand this theme and explain what the resurrection is like.

7 | The Resurrection And The Perpetual Movement Of Abundance.

> But someone will say, "How are the dead raised up? And with what body do they come?"
>
> Foolish one, what you sow is not made alive unless it dies.
>
> | 1 Corinthians 15:35-36

According to this word, if I try to attain the resurrection, I need to understand how to die. God wants to resurrect all things. After man's fall, the whole earth entered into a state of death. Therefore, God is not only interested in man's soul and body, but in everything that has fallen into this state. He wants us to fully enter into the resurrection dimension, the Kingdom of God, where all things are added unto us and where all possibilities and designs can descend from the invisible to the visible.

> But seek first the kingdom of God and His righteousness, and all these things shall be added to you.
>
> **| Matthew 6:33**

It is when we enter-in by faith into His Kingdom, His righteousness, and that coming age, that every perfect gift, every blessing, every glorious design, and every provision starts to gravitate towards us.

But unless we willingly die to our earthly things and material possessions, they cannot be quickened. As we just read, Fool, what you sow cannot be quickened back to life unless it first die.

The principle of giving and sowing work, but we cannot enter **into the state of a perpetual movement of abundance** unless we first die to all that we have.

This is the cornerstone of being a true disciple and what opens up the dimensions of God's riches, spiritual and material. It is those who follow after Jesus forsaking everything, that will perpetually possess all things.

> If anyone comes to Me and does not hate his father and mother, wife and children, brothers and sisters, yes, and his own life also, he cannot be My disciple.
>
> **| Luke 14:26**

> And everyone who has left houses or brothers or sisters or father or mother or wife or children or lands, for My name's sake, shall receive a hundredfold, and inherit eternal life.
>
> **| Matthew 19:29**

A true disciple of Jesus Christ must follow Him in such a way that neither family nor worldly possessions, nor the security of his own life can stand in the way of what God wants to do in him. This is because there will be dilemmas in life where God puts us in crossroads where we will have to choose between Him or any of these other things that make up our life in this world.

If He is not our priority in everything, He cannot conform us into His image, nor can He protect what we love. We'll be continually stripping away His Lordship, trying to protect our families, our positions, our treasures, and our lives in our own strength. We'll be pulled back and forth without ever finding His will or His ways.

Once you have made that determination by giving Jesus complete Lordship over your life, you can begin to be discipled by Him. And the first thing He does is to train us to walk in His dimension of rest and resurrection, because it is only in this spiritual dimension that everything was activated before the foundation of the world.

He doesn't have to do anything to provide for you, heal you, or give you your dreams, because He already did it. We are the ones that need to enter into that place where everything is provided and continually supplied because He has already given us His Kingdom, the inheritance by which we have all things.

This is why Paul prayed for the eyes of our understanding to be opened, to see the riches of His Glory, which is our inheritance. We receive this through the power of the resurrection that raised Christ from the dead. My prayer is that we see Christ as our head, with every power and principality under our feet, and ourselves as His divine body –the fullness of Him that fills all in all.[21]

This is what God spoke through the prophet Hosea, *on the third day we will rise again.*[22]

When Christ rose, and the saints came out of their tombs, not only did they rise, but the power and dimension of the resurrection opened up for us to live by it. This is the power that overcomes all things.

8 | How Will The Dead Be Resurrected?

Once again, taking up at the passage of scripture in Corinthians where Paul talks about how the resurrection would take place, he says:

> And what you sow, you do not sow that body that shall be, but mere grain — perhaps wheat or

[21] - Ephesians 1:17-23

[22] - Hosea 6:2

> some other grain. But God gives it a body as He pleases, and to each seed its own body.
>
> **| 1 Corinthians 15:37-38**

Our body here on Earth is a seed. It's not what will emerge in the resurrection. In other words, I will not have the same countenance nor my same body because one thing is the shape of the seed and another the shape of the tree that emerges from it. That is why God calls us "the planting of the Lord", and these trees are the sons of the resurrection, whose power causes everything to be restored, to quicken, and resurrect.

> …That they may be called trees of righteousness, the planting of the Lord, that He may be glorified." And they shall rebuild the old ruins, they shall raise up the former desolations, and they shall repair the ruined cities, the desolations of many generations.
>
> **| Isaiah 61:3b-4**

Paul now speaks about the different types of bodies in the resurrection and the contrast between our natural life and resurrected one.

> And so, it is written, "The first man Adam became a living being." The last Adam became a life-giving spirit.
>
> However, the spiritual is not first, but the natural, and afterward the spiritual.

> The first man was of the earth, made of dust; the second Man is the Lord from heaven.
>
> As was the man of dust, so also are those who are made of dust; and as is the heavenly Man, so also are those who are heavenly.
>
> **| 1 Corinthians 15:45-48**

Is it really possible for our fallen humanity to enter into such glory levels to be conformed and be in the likeness of the Heavenly One?

Yes, absolutely! Because everything spoken in Heaven is fulfilled. Christ's design is to be united as one with His sons and daughters. ***If the head is Heavenly, then so must the body be heavenly also.***

> And as we have borne the image of the man of dust, we shall also bear the image of the heavenly Man.
>
> Behold, I tell you a mystery: We shall not all sleep, but we shall all be transformed.
>
> **| 1 Corinthians 15:49 & 51**

Paul believed that not everyone was going to die. That there would be some people, those counted as worthy of attaining the resurrection power in life, who would be transformed and transferred to their eternal habitations. And this is accessible to all who can believe.

Paul wholeheartedly believed that being clothed in our heavenly habitation could invade our physical being in such a way that it reaches a point where it no longer gets corrupted, sick, or old. This is the Gospel of the Glory of Christ, who is the image of God and whose Light is veiled in the understanding of those who do not believe.[23]

This is the life-changing Gospel of Jesus Christ, the good news of the Kingdom where all things are possible.

> For this corruptible must put on incorruption, and this mortal must put on immortality. So when this corruptible has put on incorruption, and this mortal has put on immortality, then shall be brought to pass the saying that is written: "Death is swallowed up in victory." "O death, where is your sting?
>
> O Hades, where is your victory?"

| 1 Corinthians 15:54-55

Paul is speaking precisely about that for which he was groaning: To be clothed with his heavenly habitation so that everything mortal, in him, is consumed by life.

As we penetrate further and further into the heavenly city, by faith, this will become one of the most powerful spiritual exercises in which we die to our human reasoning and to all that is of this world. This is where we conquer every affliction we will ever have, with our life in Christ and the power of the resurrection. It is also how we press

---

[23] - Paraphrasing 2 Corinthians 4:4

on in our own lives until we conquer everything mortal within us. The resurrected life of Christ has the power to consume everything related to death! See it, believe it, cherish it, be determined, and overcome!

> You will also declare a thing, and it will be established for you; so light will shine on your ways.
>
> **| Job 22:28**

When Paul sought this power of the resurrection, he asked Jesus to let him know Him in the fellowship of His sufferings, even to become like Him in his death. This is because there is a victory in every affliction, and as we conquer each and every one, resurrection is being established in us.

> ... strengthening the souls of the disciples, exhorting them to continue in the faith, and saying, "We must through many tribulations enter the kingdom of God."
>
> **| Acts 14:22**

Every suffering leads us to die to something within ourselves so that the glory of Jesus Christ is established in our lives.

It is not about longing to fall prey to awful things. But when God decides to illuminate, through a circumstance, something that is off in our life, it's the perfect opportunity to bring something to death to manifest His perfection in us.

And this is how Paul sums up the truth about the resurrection consuming him:

> But thanks be to God, who gives us the victory through our Lord Jesus Christ.
>
> **| 1 Corinthians 15:57**

When you read these things, don't think that they are an impossible or difficult feat to attain. Jesus did not come to preach a gospel that was so complicated that only a few chosen ones could fulfill it. This is something much more feasible and accessible than we can imagine. But it, simply, has not been preached and believed in the right way.

THOSE WHO EXIST IN SPLENDOR

Chapter 3

We have been training in the resurrection principles, and now we are going to understand who we are in the heavenly places. God is manifesting to those who seek Him. And this isn't just about reading a book or listening to a teaching, but about taking His principles and penetrate those Godly spheres that lead us to truly know Him.

1 | Think Attentively On Heaven

The greater light I have, the more range of vision I will obtain. In these time, it is far too important to have an adequate and powerful field of vision, a heavenly perspective. Because a lack of it can easily lead to great worry and affliction about the things that transpire in the world.

There are significant conflicts on the horizon coming over the earth. So, if my focus is on this world, I will likely suffer the onslaught of many tribulations.

It's extremely relevant to understand the moment we are living in.

The Lord told me: Do not ignore the wiles of the devil but set your focus on Heaven above.

If I compare what the devil wants to do and his works with God's greatness, the enemy has absolutely nothing, meaning that the smart decision is to set our focus on His Heavenly designs.

I want us to look at a passage in the Book of Enoch, which parallels a portion of scripture where the Apostle Paul speaks about this very subject.

> Contemplate Heaven, all you sons of Heaven, and all the works of the Most High, and fear Him, and do not do evil in front of Him.
>
> | **Enoch 101:1**

> If then you were raised with Christ, seek those things which are above, where Christ is, sitting at the right hand of God. Set your mind on things above, not on things on the earth.
>
> | **Colossians 3:1-2**

Enoch emphasizes that we should focus carefully, put all out attention on heaven, and adds:

> Wherefore fear not, ye that have suffered;
> For healing shall be your portion,
>
> **| Enoch 96:3a**

God wants us to take our sight off the schemes and conflicts being plotted down here on Earth.

> and a bright light will shine upon you, and the Voice of Rest you will hear from Heaven.
>
> **| Enoch 96:3b**

This is where we have to set our focus, hence the insistence on us knowing our Light nature.

Imagine that you are in an old, dark house and you can't see a thing. Suddenly, you hear the sound of roaches and rats, and it scares you. You ask yourself where will they come from? You light a match, and with this small flicker, you try to locate where they are. This is similar to what Christianity is like today.

There is no way to know and undo the devil's plans from an earthly perspective of darkness. We might find a mouse and kill it, great! But what would happen if we were to connect to the home's main light switch? Instantly, once you turn it on, the whole house would be flooded with light.

Who's going to be more stressed then, us or the rats and the roaches?

The latter, of course; because once you connect to the Light source, you already have the victory. Every hollow and hiding place, where they once hid, will be exposed to the Light. And this is the true gospel of the Kingdom. Heaven's master light switch that illuminates the whole earth is the City of the Living God, the New Jerusalem which Jesus established, through His resurrection, on God's Holy Mount.

> No one, when he has lit a lamp, puts it in a secret place or under a basket, but on a lampstand, that those who come in may see the light.
>
> **| Luke 11:33**

God certainly didn't hide the supreme light that beams more than the sun and moon, but He placed it on His Holy Mount to shine upon all men.

Something vital that we need to understand about this, and I want you to engrave this in your heart:

If I carefully focus my attention on Heaven, that is where my consciousness and level of light are going to be.

But if I focus on sickness, the virus, fear that has been unleashed on the planet, the problems that I am going through, and what the end of the world will be like, that will also be reflected in my level of consciousness my level of light. Unfortunately, if this is my focus, it will be quite far from being the light; it is only darkness.

But, if my full attention is on heaven, all of my needs will be abundantly supplied, just as Jesus said: *Seek ye first the kingdom of God and His righteousness, and all these things shall be added to you.*[24]

2 | The City of the Living God

Now, let's see how the City of God, the New Jerusalem is the very Kingdom of God that Jesus brought to Earth, the city that ancient heroes of faith saw and cherished, but which God has now given it to us. It is where our identity as sons of God and citizens of Heaven lies.

Concerning this, the author of Hebrews writes:

> By faith Abraham obeyed when he was called to go out to the place which he would receive as an inheritance. And he went out, not knowing where he was going.
>
> By faith he dwelt in the land of promise as in a foreign country, dwelling in tents with Isaac and Jacob, the heirs with him of the same promise;
>
> **for he waited for the city which has foundations, whose builder and maker is God.**
>
> These all died in faith, not having received the promises, but having seen them afar off were assured of them, embraced them and confessed that they were strangers and pilgrims on the earth.
>
> For those who say such things declare plainly that they seek a homeland.

---

[24] - Matthew 6:33

> And truly if they had called to mind that country from which they had come out, they would have had opportunity to return.
>
> But now they desire a better, that is, a heavenly country. Therefore, God is not ashamed to be called their God, for He has prepared a city for them.
>
> | **Hebrews 11:8-10 & 13-16**

braham entered the Promised Land, received it as an inheritance, attained immeasurable wealth, was given the power to defeat his enemies, to know and honor the high priest Melchizedek, and was revealed the law of God by divine inspiration. Yet, despite all this, he never set his sight on the Earth, choosing instead to continually set his gaze on the Heavens, seeking the Heavenly City.

This phrase: Therefore, God is not ashamed to be called their God, implies that there are those of whom He is ashamed and others of whom He feels honored. The latter are those who have set their sight on the City of Light.

The new covenant and the work of Jesus Christ in man is the most glorious mystery a human mind is capable of understanding.

The Old Covenant was external –God dwelt outside of man– but the New Covenant is internal. God made us his tabernacle and placed His laws in our hearts. In His immeasurable greatness, He has put, by His Spirit, everything heavenly within the heart of his children.

The extraordinary thing about all this is that we don't just have a little piece of God, but we have all of Him. Yes, the entire universe, His whole Kingdom, dwells within us. How this mighty wonder takes place, is what we will now develop step by step.

Just as the New Covenant varies from the Old Covenant by one being internal and the other external, the two cities –the earthly and the Heavenly– also differ in their fundamental essence. The Heavenly is above the earthly. And when that which is from Heaven is established, what is from the Earth becomes obsolete. God no longer dwells in the Ark of the Covenant; the Heavenly Ark took its place within the Most High. Thus, the earthly Jerusalem ceases from being the center of divine activity, to give place to the heavenly one. The first one is local, situated within Israel's territory, and it is for the Jews. But the second one is global, spanning the entire Earth, and it is designed for Jews and Greeks alike, and every other nationality in the world.

The New Jerusalem becomes visible, or palpable, on the Earth as her Sons embrace it, conceive it, and are nurtured by her.

In other words, the more real the New Jerusalem becomes in my life, the more I understand it, and the more I will bring her down from Heaven to Earth.

If I try to conceive the New Jerusalem with my natural mind, I'll imagine it as something physical, like a beautiful city on Earth filled with glory and splendor. But that is just an earthly, three-dimensional way of thinking and that we use to see all things.

The New Jerusalem is not of this earth, but it is in our midst. It is invisible to our natural eyes, but powerfully real to our spiritual senses.

Adam was created in the City of God; the garden was a part of it. He lived in it, experienced it, enjoyed its rivers, ate its fruits, from the eternal Tree of Life.

John the apostle saw the New Jerusalem when he was taken up into heaven to see the great Kingdom mysteries. He was in a dimension that has no time, and he saw what Adam lived.

We can clearly see in the Epistle to the Hebrews how we have been given this city, to enter in it and enjoy it now.

> But you have come to Mount Zion and to the city of the living God, the heavenly Jerusalem, to an innumerable company of angels,
>
> to the general assembly and church of the firstborn who are registered in heaven, to God the Judge of all, to the spirits of just men made perfect,
>
> to Jesus the Mediator of the new covenant, and to the blood of sprinkling that speaks better things than that of Abel.
>
> **| Hebrews 12:22-24**

When it says that we have come, it does not mean that we are separated from all these things, waiting to see when we can enter and enjoy them, but rather, it implies what has been given to us. At the end of this passage in Scripture, we see another example where we have come to Jesus and His precious blood. However, once again, it does not mean that we are near Him, the reality is He dwells in us, the same as His blood.

But instead, he is saying that through Jesus and His precious blood, we can enter in and have access to all these things. All these angels are part of the Heavenly city that opens its doors for us.

The Heavenly Jerusalem is in the midst of us. It is made up of all the Saints of every generation. All of them alive, both those who have been and those that are to come. For God is not the God of the dead but the living, for all live to Him.[25] Furthermore, the city is filled with angels that serve and minister to all its citizens.

Within it we also find the throne of justice, from where the Father judges the whole Earth and the blood of Jesus that mercifully reaches out to all who are to be saved.

God has allowed me to enter and walk around the city, in the heavenly spheres, on several occasions.

The city isn't like an earthly metropolis that exists on a single three-dimensional plane, but it has infinite internal doors that lead to God's knowledge, and each one opens up to places that can only be seen and understood from that dimension. Enoch could see the various heavens from this city. Job could see the place of Light and the dwelling place of wisdom. There, is where we find the storehouses of all divine provision, the treasures of snow and hail, the ordering of the innumerable and diverse classes of angels. In its midst is the great throne of God, the Heavenly eternal Ark not made by hands, the great court of Divine Justice. Paradise is in it and emits its reflection on earth for the sons of Light to perceive it and find their rest in it.

In the place of wisdom within the holy city, we find the great eternal library with the books of Heaven and all

[25] - Luke 20:38

the knowledge that we can receive. We can also have access to the languages of Heaven and Earth, and every witty invention and technology that has been, and will be revealed to men on Earth by His grace and power alone.

The whole city activates when we enter it in the Spirit. Moreover, the city is the realm where we can be transferred from one place to another, physically or spiritually. It is the city that allowed Ezekiel to be taken in the Spirit, by a lock of hair, to see the earthly Jerusalem and the abominations committed in the temple.

There are doors inside the city, which, unlike our own, they look like atmospheres or subtle veils of luminous gases one can pass from one to another. They are entrances to dimensions such as those experienced by John when he was taken up to Heaven. He was before the throne and was then taken to a place in front of the sea. Afterward, he was brought to a site where the sea was of glass and fire, and from there he transferred up to Mount Zion. God took Him from one place to another because the city isn't static but is in continuous movement revealing different places, treasures, and secrets of the Living God.

Phillip was supernaturally transferred from Ethiopia to Jerusalem because he entered the city. More than once, Elijah was translated to heaven and then back to earth and from one place to another by chariots of fire because he understood how transportation operates within the city.

Paul could be in one location and be with the brethren in another distant place because they lived within the city's dimension.

> For though I am absent in the flesh, yet I am with you in spirit, rejoicing to see your good order and the steadfastness of your faith in Christ.
>
> **| Colossians 2:5**

All these things seem unusual and alien to our 21st. Century reality, but in fact, they are not. Jesus told His disciples that the least in the Kingdom of God was greater than all the prophets in the Old Testament. That implies being greater than Elijah, Moses, and all the rest.

Beloved, these things are happening today. We all qualify to be the least in the Kingdom. God is only looking for those who are willing to believe Him at His Word.

We have both seen and experienced these types of miracles several times in our lifetime, and we are not unique. The same thing can happen to you.

When Heaven reveals itself, allowing us to see a vision, access the place of His wisdom and receive a foreign language or entire careers, or see the throne of His judgments, it's because we are entering the city. When God allows us to see angels or the unexplained multiplication of our possessions, or experience something from Heaven on Earth, it is because the city is manifesting before us.

The city is the place where God rules over the Earth. Every time something supernatural happens in our life, it happens because we have made an intermittence in the city. It is how we receive the most extraordinary creative miracles.

But God is calling us not just to enter it occasionally but to become pillars within His temple and gates between Heaven and Earth.

> That books will be given to the righteous and wise, and will be a source of joy, and uprightness, and much wisdom. And books will be given to them, and they will believe in them, and rejoice over them; and all the righteous, who have learnt from them all the ways of truth, will be recompensed.
>
> **| Enoch 103:12-13**

It is there that you will find the mansions of the luminaries and those of the saints, the stores of heavenly weapons, treasures, as well as the stores of organs and heavenly medicinal plants.

I recall, on one occasion, I was in Germany with other spiritual brethren, mostly apostles and prophets, twelve in all.

For three days, we gathered together and entered the dimensions of the Spirit. Each day we experienced a deep silence and a peace that joined us together as one mind and one soul. We all thought and felt the same thing at precisely the same time. It was quite unique and incomprehensible. When the angels worshiped in our midst, all of us in one voice joined into to sing the same melody, in the same tone, ending at precisely the same time. It was as if an invisible baton orchestrated our voices with its tempos. We were stunned by the perfect unity.

By the third day, all of us appeared in the heavenly city as if one and the same. It was glorious, full of the sons of God, all of them luminous; angels walked among them, others flew. The whole city shone. Its river waters were like liquid gold full of light and colors. The Tree of Life was like many trees joined together to form a single trunk with branches full of lush foliage, all of them gleaming like gold and diamonds with fire, with every leaf emitting light. It was majestic, teeming with glowing colors that varied, and filled the garden's center.

As we beheld the beauty before us, a great commotion was heard. From every part of the city, hundreds arrived from the cloud of witnesses, rejoicing and shouting with sheer delight at the sight of us: "They finally got it, they finally came in."

I will never forget their looks of utter joy. Our understanding completely shifted. We knew we had penetrated something that would only increase and pave the way for millions more to enter.

Paul compares the heavenly and earthly cities to Sarah and Hagar. The first one is free, representing the city of the Spirit because where the Spirit of the Lord is, there is liberty[26]. The second One is a bondwoman who is under the law and the flesh[27].

Now, the free woman differs entirely from the slave, and they cannot combine with one and the other. In the City of God there is no difference between its inhabitants, Jews, Greeks or whatever nationality, because everyone is clothed in the new man, after the image of the One who created them.

[26] - 2 Corinthians 3:17

[27] - Galatians 4:24-30

> Where there is neither Greek nor Jew, circumcised nor uncircumcised, barbarian, Scythian, slave nor free, but Christ is all and in all.
>
> | Colossians 3:11

3 | The Wife Of The Lamb

Entering the New Jerusalem first has to do with understanding who we are as the wife of the Lamb. Marriage on Earth is the union of two souls, two bodies, and two spirits that become one, the same flesh. In a spiritual sense, the mystical marriage of Christ with His church is the union of God's Spirit with the spirit of man.

This is why the Scripture says:

> For no one ever hated his own flesh, but nourishes and cherishes it, just as the Lord does the church.
>
> For we are members of His body, of His flesh and of His bones.
>
> "For this reason, a man shall leave his father and mother and be joined to his wife, and the two shall become one flesh."
>
> This is a great mystery, **but I speak concerning Christ and the church.**
>
> | Ephesians 5:29-32

Paul also says concerning this:

> But he who is joined to the Lord is one spirit with Him.
>
> **| 1 Corinthians 6:17**

The only way to be the Body of Christ, members of His flesh and bones, is by being His wife.

4 | The City Descends To Earth

Bear in mind that there is no time in the heavenly and spiritual spheres, which is why when John saw the Heavenly Jerusalem, he was witnessing the glorious moment when Jesus unites with His nascent church, to inhabit it and become one with it.

This is precisely what happened in the Upper Room on the Day of Pentecost, with one hundred and twenty men and women gathered together in one accord.

> When the Day of Pentecost had fully come, they were **all with one accord** in one place. And suddenly there came a sound from heaven, as of a rushing mighty wind, and it filled the whole house where they were sitting. Then there appeared to them divided tongues, as of fire, and one sat upon each of them. And they were all filled with the Holy Spirit
>
> **| Acts 2:1-4**

This is the first time God came to dwell in His people and make His tabernacle in those who believe on His Name.

It's in this sublime moment that we are completely filled, saturated, and clothed in the Spirit of God to become members of His body, his flesh, and his bones.[28].

The Body of Christ isn't a religious organization, but it is the vital and sovereign union of these two spirits. Only the wife has the right to the deepest level of intimacy with Christ and once filled with this matchless, immeasurable love, she will long to submit entirely to the Lord as her head.

This is because only the wife is genuinely committed, not the bride.

This has also resulted in most of the church embracing a way of thinking and acting vastly different from the Mind of Christ.

> There are sixty queens and eighty concubines, and virgins without number. My dove, my perfect one, is the only one.
>
> The daughters saw her and called her blessed, the queens and the concubines, and they praised her.
>
> **| Song of Solomon 6:8-9b**

There is a divine call being uttered right now, similar to the word in Revelation: The Spirit and the spouse say come. The New Jerusalem is calling her children. The wife also has the power to call and the position to draw those who will be the true Sons of the Most High.

The light of the New Jerusalem must now illuminate the

---

[28] Ephesians 5:30-31

Earth, and Heaven urges to do so, which is why it paused the whole church worldwide. (2020 Pandemic)

5 | The Wife's Unanimity

One morning, before sunrise, I saw the power of the Body of Christ united in the Father. It was like the sum of all the lights that we are, each of us becoming a laser beam that forms within Him. This power contains the prayers of those in unity. When any one of us makes a prayer request, it passes through that unity, the laser, and is energized within the Father, causing an immediate reply. Jesus operated in that power, from that oneness in the Father.

The body is one within Jesus, and Jesus within the Father, all fused together. It is the reason why Jesus insisted on teaching that He and the Father were one. And it is from this oneness that the Father, in Him, did all the works.

The same thing applies now with His body, His children, those who have turned to the Father.

All of creation is united in the Father so that it responds to the manifestation of the sons; because they manifest the Father.

Unity is the power that draws others into the Father, for the Father is ONE.

> …that they all may be one, as You, Father, are in Me, and I in You; that they also may be one in Us, that the world may believe that You sent

> Me. And the glory which You gave Me I have given them, that they may be one just as We are one:
>
> | **John 17:21-22**

ONE is the unifying nature of the Father. **To know the Father is to know His Oneness.** Those who knows Him cannot live in separation, cannot endure it. They are deeply hurt by it, as is the Father, which is why they seek to unite in Him.

True unity can only begin in the Spirit. In the soul, each head is its own world, impossible to unify. The soul can enjoy bonds of social unity but cannot, of itself, achieve oneness, for it can only come from the Father. Only the Lord can bring together every piece and every joint, forming the perfect edifice.

Only when we know the Father in His nature of oneness can we truly come to know ourselves and recognize the same nature of God in others. We are then able to see the image of Christ in each other.

This is the reason why it was so crucial for them to be in the Upper Room, in one accord, to receive the Spirit of the Father and the power that would endow them to change the world.

When we come together as one, by the Father's love bonds, we become those that shall build the old waste places; the ones that raise up the foundations of many generations; We will then be called repairers of the breach, and restorers of streets to dwell in.[29] It is in this unity that God's mysteries are revealed to us.

[29] Isaiah 58:12 Paraphrased

That their hearts may be encouraged, **being knit together in love**, and attaining to all riches of the full assurance of understanding, to the knowledge of the mystery of God, both of the Father and of Christ, in whom are hidden all the treasures of wisdom and knowledge.

| Colossians 2:2-3

Chapter 4

THE TABERNACLE OF GOD WITH MEN

1 | Mount Zion

The Book of Daniel tells us about the time when the prophet interpreted King Nebuchadnezzar's dream. He saw a large rock fall from Heaven, striking the image the king had seen in his dreams. The statute's feet symbolized the Roman Empire, and the rock is obviously Christ, who came down from Heaven to destroy this empire in the 1st. Century.

> Then the iron, the clay, the bronze, the silver, and the gold were crushed together, and became like

> chaff from the summer threshing floors; the wind carried them away so that no trace of them was found. And the stone that struck the image became a great mountain and filled the whole earth.
>
> **| Daniel 2:35**

Christ was the Rock, Israel's stumbling stone, that turned into the great Mount Zion covering the entire earth. And it's precisely upon this great mountain, which is Christ Himself, that the great city of the living God is seated.

> And he carried me away in the Spirit **to a great and high mountain**, and showed me the great city, the holy Jerusalem, descending out of heaven from God,
>
> **| Revelation 21:10**

Here, John is seeing the heavenly city descending from Heaven, but he also states that it descends from God. The city was in God and descended from Him to make His tabernacle among men.

> Then I, John, saw the holy city, the New Jerusalem, coming down out of heaven from God, prepared as a bride adorned for her husband. And I heard a loud voice from heaven saying, **"Behold, the tabernacle of God is with men**, and He will dwell with them, and they shall be His people. God Himself will be with them and be their God".
>
> **| Revelation 21:2-3**

It clearly states here that the New Jerusalem is God's tabernacle with men.

Now, it is common knowledge that we are the temple of the Holy Spirit and that God dwells within us. However, due to false theologies, the New Jerusalem was separated from God's dwelling place within us. This way of thinking has robbed the church of its greatest heavenly blessings.

> He who overcomes shall inherit all things, and I will be his God and he shall be My son.
>
> **| Revelation 21:7**

> Who are those that will inherit the things of the Spirit? The Sons of the freewoman! The Sons of the Heavenly City.
>
> Now we, brethren, as Isaac was, are children of promise.
>
> But, as he who was born according to the flesh then persecuted him who was born according to the Spirit, even so it is now.
>
> Nevertheless, what does the Scripture say? "Cast out the bondwoman and her son, *for the son of the bondwoman shall not be heir with the son of the freewoman.*"
>
> **| Galatians 4:28-30**

The religious system awaiting the Earth's destruction for the New Jerusalem to descend definitely cannot inherit the things that God has for us since this is a privilege that only the "freewoman" has.

Throw out the bondwoman! It is a decisive action because the slave cannot inherit with the freewoman. This means to cast out every system of bondage out of our life. The way we navigate in a merit system, our work, our efforts, the price we have paid, the pride we take in building a church, the money we have given, the hours we pray every day, etc., it all comes out to law, religion, and death. When we change our relationship with God, from receiving directly from His Spirit to receiving from man what we should know in God, we become a slave to the system. As servants of God, we can give you many wonderful things, but we must never, ever take the place of God in your life.

Throw it all out, says the Lord! Because it has nothing to do with the Spirit of liberty that proceeds from our union with Christ, which is the "freewoman!"

Every way of thinking that binds you to the Earth and this world's system, throw it out. Everything that leads you to think that God needs to act from an external form cast it out! Because the New Covenant has nothing to do with the old one. But it has to do with God revealing Himself in our hearts and us living through Him. Thus, our life in God can be summed up not by what we do but in who we are.

2 | The Free One Has The Glory Of God

> And he carried me away in the Spirit to a great and high mountain, and showed me the great city, the holy Jerusalem, descending out of

> heaven from God, **having the glory of God**. Her light was like a most precious stone, like a jasper stone, clear as crystal.
>
> | **Revelation 21:10-11**

Here we see that God's design consists not only of Him justifying us but also of Him glorifying us.

> For whom He foreknew, He also predestined to be conformed to the image of His Son, that He might be the firstborn among many brethren. Moreover, whom He predestined, these He also called; whom He called, these He also justified; and whom He justified, **these He also glorified**.
>
> | **Romans 8:29-30**

This glorification is the entry point into the New Jerusalem, which is not something external but internal.

This glory is the very Holy Spirit dwelling in us. **To the extent that I understand the Kingdom of God, the heavenly dimensions, and the fullness of the inheritance that I have been given, I will also discover the measure of the Holy Spirit I have been given as well.**

We discover the fullness of the Holy Spirit within us, to the degree that we come to know God and His Kingdom.

A limited understanding of the Kingdom of God will produce lesser manifestations of the Holy Spirit. In contrast, a broader knowledge of the Kingdom of God will open in me the unlimited dimensions of the Holy Spirit. This goes far beyond exercising the gifts of the Spirit, for the gifts are one thing, and the one who gives them, the Spirit is another.

Notice in the following passage how glorification and the outpouring of the Holy Spirit are intimately linked.

> He who believes in Me, as the Scripture has said, out of his heart will flow rivers of living water." But this He spoke concerning the Spirit, whom those believing in Him would receive; for **the Holy Spirit was not yet given, because Jesus was not yet glorified.**
>
> | John 7:38-39

Afterward, once Jesus was glorified in His Kingdom, He poured out the Spirit of His own glory, which is what we receive as an inheritance.

3 | Change Of An Era

We saw how the Old Covenant is external, and the New Covenant is internal. When God speaks about establishing a new covenant, He says it would be entirely different from the previous one. And this new covenant consists of God writing His laws in our hearts.

This is very important for us to understand because fifty days after the Passover –when Moses left Egypt with the people of Israel– Mount Sinai filled with fire and smoke and lightning. It is when God wrote the tables of the law on stone.

Moreover, it's also a type and a shadow of what would happen on the Day of Pentecost with the outpouring of the Holy Spirit, since we see the same symbols manifest: fire, a strong rushing wind, and the Earth shaking.

So when the Holy Spirit descended fifty days after the Ascension, God printed His laws in the heart of men. And it is from this moment on that the temple of God was established within humankind.

You see, God has always spoken about a remnant, which in this case means being called from Mount Zion in the Heavenly city, for it is on this mountain that we find God's authority and the Kingdom of the Living God.

I want you to see now how Pentecost, in the first century, brought a complete change of era, just like when the tables of the law were written on Mount Sinai, for that is the moment when the Mosaic Era began.

And once again, it's clear that we are entering a change in era at this moment of history. From the youngest to the oldest, everyone can feel a radical change coming on our planet.

4 | The Fruit Of Glorification

Now, let us see now how our glorification is carried out.

All of God's plan is aimed at glorifying His children: *whom*

He called, these He also justified; and whom He justified, these He also glorified.

This was written because God wants the glory of Jesus Christ seen on the Earth through a remnant. These are the offspring of the Spirit, the Sons of the Spiritual Jerusalem, the mother of us all.

Let's take a closer look at one chapter in the Bible that deals with the glorification of the sons of Light, as revealed to the prophet Isaiah.

> Arise, shine; for your light has come! And the glory of the Lord is risen upon you.
>
> **| Isaiah 60:1**

The light mentioned here is nothing other than the Light and glory of Jesus Christ dwelling in us, but God wants us to experience the full extension of what this glorification means for us that are alive in this world.

It has been mistakenly preached that we are justified here on Earth, only to be glorified after death. However, this is so far from the reality that Christ came to bring us.

When the Lord speaks about the New Jerusalem in the book of Revelation, He says that there will be saved nations that will bring His glory to her.

> And the nations of those who are saved shall walk in its light, and the kings of the earth bring their glory and honor into it.

> Its gates shall not be shut at all by day (there shall be no night there). And they shall bring the glory and the honor of the nations into it.
>
> **| Revelation 21:24-26**

If Jesus in His glory speaks to us about nations that will be saved, He is also implying that there will be other nations that will not be saved. Otherwise, He would simply say that every nation shall bring their glory to the New Jerusalem.

This scenario can only take place on Earth, for it is the only place where we find differences between nations. Besides the city of God manifests in the midst of these, causing them to recognize her and bring their riches and glory to her. Thus, we see the existance of a Heavenly city amid a physical, natural world.

It has been taught that the Earth needs to be destroyed for the New Jerusalem to manifest. But this is opposite to what Jesus, who is the Spirit of prophecy, teaches.

> But there shall by no means enter it anything that defiles, or causes an abomination or a lie, but only those who are written in the Lamb's Book of Life.
>
> **| Revelation 21:27**

A statute or a law exists whenever there is a possibility of someone violating it. The prohibition –denying entry of anything defiled or abominable into the city- was set in place because of the possibility of someone, with these traits, trying to enter it.

The heavenly realm, the City of the Living God, is what rules over the earth. It's a heavenly reality amid the world today, just as Babylon[30] is a city that also rules the nations in the realm of darkness.

It is essential to understand that we can only have that for which we can believe. **Our level of light will only be to the degree of our consciousness of Heaven's reality**. So, the more aware I am of God's designs in my life, the more light I will emanate.

The Book of Enoch says: *think attentively on Heaven, ye children of Heaven, and in all the work of the Most High*. The more conscious I am of this, the more I will penetrate the city's dimensions.

Just as Emerson always says, we have the world that we have believed for. If I believe in a world where I can be attacked by anything, including demons, I will likely be struck that way.

But if instead, I believe that I am surrounded by angels, I will likely see and interact with many of them.

It takes the same amount of work to believe that you are surrounded by demons as it does to believe that you are surrounded by angels. Because just as hell has invaded Earth, Heaven has also done so at a more powerful level.

The Lord wants to show us here that the New Jerusalem is indeed the Tabernacle of God with men, Christ, and the Father dwelling within the believer. He in us, and we in Him. The city in us, and we in the city.

[30] - Revelation 17:18

> Now I saw a new heaven and a new earth, for the first heaven and the first earth had passed away. Also, there was no more sea.
>
> Then I, John, saw the holy city, New Jerusalem, coming down out of heaven from God, prepared as a bride adorned for her husband.
>
> And I heard a loud voice from heaven saying, "Behold, the tabernacle of God is with men, and He will dwell with them, and they shall be His people. God Himself will be with them and be their God.

| Revelation 21:1-3

If I read this first verse with the natural mind, my reasoning will lead me to think that it refers to a new planet set to exist in the distant future. But what God is really talking about here is His divine manifestation, that was coming to change all things.

When God speaks of a new heaven and a new earth, he's referring to the fact that before Christ came in the flesh, the heavens and the Earth were in complete darkness because of God's separation with man. Each of us has come to a world which God has filled with His Glory for the past 2000 years. However, this was not the case before Christ.

The devil had dominion and control over the entire planet. Heaven and Earth were in total disunity, and the throne of Jesus Christ was empty as King. This, however, radically changed when Jesus ascended into the heavens and took His seat as Majesty on high. At that moment, the darkness-filled Earth that existed before Jesus Christ ceased to exist. And according to scripture, today, we have a world filled with the Glory of God.

Of course, not everyone is aware of this glory that exists everywhere. But when our spirit awakens, we realize that it really is here.

We need to understand that Heaven with an empty throne is not the same as Heaven with Christ seated as King of Kings and Lord of Lords, reigning over all the Earth. **Everything, and I mean absolutely everything, changed with the resurrection and ascension of Jesus Christ.**

> Jesus says: "Come to know what is in front of you, and that which is hidden from you will become clear to you. For there is nothing hidden that will not become manifest."
>
> **| Thomas 5 (Apocryphal)**

Once we are awakened, we can see as Heaven sees, and the invisible is revealed before our very eyes.

For years, I have been going to the beach to watch the sunrise because there are things that happen at that time in the morning that cannot be seen once the sun is out.

There's a moment when all focus is on Him. Nothing else is heard, not the birds, not the ocean waves, not wind, nothing. Everything takes second place, and the only thing that captures your sight is the sublime majesty that begins to fill everything with its Light. Some see a sunrise, and some see beyond the visible or the obvious –God's eternal greatness lavishing His riches in glory.

On one occasion, I went to the beach one afternoon, and as I walked by the shore, I saw a barren field among the dunes. The Spirit led me to enter through a small path that opened up among the high mounds of sand and grass. As I walked in, it was like a large pot full of wildflowers. I felt a sense of infinite peace. Suddenly, the Lord shone in all creation, radiating light in everything, the flowers, the butterflies, the sand, the shells. The grass gleamed like crystal gold. Everything was simply beautiful, the soft breeze blowing and the sand under my feet. Then, I clearly understood, that in Him we move and live and have our being. All creation reveals Him and is the visible fruit of his amazing love and glory with which He made all things.

All of Creation was meticulously thought out and sprung forth from the heart of God to bear His seal and His unfathomable wisdom.

As an artist, I know that a part of me remains in each one of my artworks. The same thing happens with each of God's greatest and smallest creations. Part of His mind and soul is imprinted within each one of them.

The Sea No Longer Existed

Let's look back at the passage from Revelation 19.

When we read these scriptures, written from a heavenly dimension, we can never fully embrace what it means with our natural mind and a three-dimensional kind of understanding.

When God says that the sea no longer exists, He's referring to a spiritual region, from where the beast of the book of Revelation emerges[31], and also the waters where the "Great Harlot" sits,[32] not the oceans on the planet.

It is also a region of death. We see this clearly in the book of Revelation when he speaks of the different areas that give up their dead.

> **The sea** gave up the dead who were in it, and **Death and Hades** delivered up the dead who were in them. And they were judged, each one according to his works.
>
> | **Revelation 20:13**

Had this word referred to the dead drowned at sea, the scripture would say: The sea gave up its dead and the land also, but he's talking about Death and Hades, revealing that the sea, along with this two, are spiritual regions and not physical places.

The problem we run into is that with the addition of the chapter titles in the Bible, the reader's mind is conditioned in a particular direction. One of these is: "A New Heaven and a New Earth."

Then, when the Apostle John talks about this new heaven and earth, he implies that death and Hades had already been judged, and together with them, this entire region that was in the sea.

At what point were death and hell defeated? In the resurrection of Jesus Christ. They were conquered in that

---

[31] Revelation 13:1

[32] Revelation 17:1

glorious act. They were stripped of all their power over the true Sons of God. It is the resurrection –the power of God– that establishes His tabernacle –the New Jerusalem– within us.

This is what the true gospel, the one that shines with the glory and the Light of Jesus Christ, which leads us to understand our salvation from God's victory, is all about.

Those of us who belong to the day and to the Light are no longer subject to an earth ruled by Death, Hades, and the waters of the deep. But instead, we are under the authority and judgment of the New Jerusalem, the city of the Living God, which is God's tabernacle in men.

Those who are of the dust descend to the dust. Those who are of the Light ascend to the Light. The dust draws its own, and the Light those who are its own. The more Light we become, the more the dust loses its power over us.

So, let's move on to know the place of our citizenship.

> But **you have come to Mount Zion and to the city of the living God, the heavenly Jerusalem,**
>
> | Hebrews 12:22

This is the glorious city of which the Prophet Isaiah spoke about. And now we will see the visible fruit of the city of Light once it manifests amid a world filled with darkness.

> For behold, the darkness shall cover the earth, and deep darkness the people. But the Lord will

> arise over you, and His glory will be seen upon you.
>
> The Gentiles shall come to your light, and kings to the brightness of your rising.
>
> | Isaiah 60:2-3

We once again see kings and nations led by a wisdom and a light different from this world. They receive what proceeds out of the New Jerusalem and walk in the light of this remnant. It is also a light of government since it has to do with kings and nations.

It has an incredible power of attraction because God's Glory is like a magnet whose power draws all things unto itself in an amazing way.

When this remnant begins to shine, it draws those whose names were written in the Lamb's Book of Life before the foundation of the world, to the city of God.

Isaiah then describes not only how His children come, but also how the abundance of riches is given to them.

> Lift up your eyes all around and see: They all gather together. They come to you. Your sons shall come from afar, and your daughters shall be nursed at your side.
>
> Then you shall see and become radiant, and your heart shall swell with joy, because the abundance of the sea shall be turned to you, the wealth of the Gentiles shall come to you.
>
> | Isaiah 60:4-5

The important thing here is not to focus on the riches, which has corrupted the church in many cases. To be the remnant, we must have wealth under our feet. The ones who have died to the system of this world are those who are part of the New Jerusalem. And as long as that death is not evident in our lives, meaning the grain has fallen to the ground and died, it cannot bear fruit, nor can we activate this level of light or this power of attraction.

He then adds, what symbolically represents the best of the offering that we are to bring to God's altar.

> All the flocks of Kedar shall be gathered together to you, the rams of Nebaioth shall minister to you. They shall ascend with acceptance on My altar, and I will glorify the house of My glory.
>
> **| Isaiah 60:7**

Obviously, once the New Jerusalem descends, there is no longer a need for the sacrifices of rams and sheep.

It's not talking about a sacrifice for the atonement of sin, but about something that is brought, that is served to us, for we are the altar in the temple. The Lord glorifies the house of His glory once we recognize what has been granted to us and truly become the sons of God.

> "Who are these who fly like a cloud, and like doves to their roosts?
>
> **| Isaiah 60:8**

Once you have the heavenly perception of the New Jerusalem, you will realize that the city sits atop the Holy

Mount, surrounded by a cloud, that hides God's mysteries.

The Word of God says that the throne of the Most High is covered by darkness, made of thick clouds.

> He made darkness His secret place; His canopy around Him was dark waters and thick clouds of the skies.
>
> **| Psalms 18:11**

Both the New Jerusalem and God's throne are protected by these clouds not to be defiled.

The phrase "who are these who fly like a cloud" refers to a dense cloud, In Hebrew is called God's Nephele[33]

On one occasion, God told me the soul is always looking for forms and that He wants us to enter the understanding of His Nephele which is void of earthly forms. He wants us to be transformed into His image having left all earthly forms behind. You see, the more we are open to change, the more we will experience God's supernatural realm.

These that fly like a cloud are the true body of Christ of all ages, present, past and future, "The timeless cloud of witnesses" on His Holy Mount. What I find interesting in this scripture is the word doves.

When I looked up the word in the original Hebrew, the Strong's Concordance led me to the term Yayin, and I was utterly surprised by its meaning. It means wine or a great feast. In other words, amid the cloud of His Presence, there is a great feast brought to these who make up the cloud of God.

[33] - Greek word meaning cloudy, or a cluster of dense clouds.

On the other hand, doves are also very symbolic in scripture. It was a dove that brought Noah the olive branch of a new world.

These doves in the account of Isaiah fly to their windows. They see both outside and inside which in a spiritual sense means they can see both dimensions.

We see the fruit of being in this cloud and on God's Holy Mount, as Isaiah goes on to say:

> Surely the coastlands shall wait for Me; and the ships of Tarshish will come first, to bring your sons from afar. Their silver and their gold with them, to the name of the Lord your God, and to the Holy One of Israel, because **He has glorified you.**
>
> | Isaiah 60:9

5 | The City Is Exclusive

Although the entire world is called to the Most High's salvation, and many accept it, entry into the heavenly city is solely for those that have washed their garments and are worthy of it.

> Blessed are those who do His commandments, that they may have the right to the Tree of Life and may enter through the gates into the city.
>
> But outside are dogs and sorcerers and sexually immoral and murderers and idolaters, and whoever loves and practices a lie.
>
> | Revelation 22:14-15

Lies are so destructive, that constitute one of the most substantial barriers to can keep you from entering and possessing all things.

We live in an era where lying has become so commonplace. Society, status, the mass media, this world's entire structure is based on a system of lies. Whoever wants to survive in this world or reach any position all too often gets caught up in a system of lies that drags them down. This world's system is ruled by the father of lies –satan. Everything in it is darkness; lies that leads to destruction, imprisoning those who practice them, and keeping them from possessing their inheritance in God.

This is why it is crucial to know the Truth and love it, understanding why we believe what we believe. This is the way to destroy every religious lying fable keeping us from knowing Christ and His Light.

Blessed are those who wash their robes. They will have the right to enter through the city's gates and eat the fruit from the Tree of Life.

> And the Spirit and the bride say, "Come!" And let him who hears say, "Come!" And let him who thirsts come. Whoever desires, let him take the water of life freely.
>
> | **Revelation 22:17**

6 | God Is Calling The Wise

Notice what the Book of Enoch says:

> And they shall be resplendent for times without number; for righteousness is the judgement of

God; for to the faithful He will give faithfulness in the habitation of upright paths. And they shall see those who were born in darkness led into darkness, while the righteous shall be resplendent. And the sinners shall cry aloud and see them resplendent, and they indeed will go where days and seasons are prescribed for them.

| **Enoch 108:14-15**

This is precisely what God is showing me by the Spirit. A group of people with understanding that penetrate the New Jerusalem. These are those who live in His splendor, the spouse of the Lamb. As a result of their entering-in, a great judgment is released upon the wickedness of the earth.

One day in the forest, while I was meditating on the Lord, I heard this word coming to me:

But all things that are exposed are made manifest by the light, for whatever makes manifest is light.

| **Ephesians 5:13**

When we first read this portion of scripture, most people believe it refers to sin or crookedness exposure. But now, let us read it from the dimension of Light.

My husband, Emerson, has been teaching us how to bring things from the invisible to the visible realm through Quantum Physics. And he has shown us that when Light is consciously observed, light waves or vibrations have the possibility of becoming physical matter. Light has the power to manifest the invisible and bring it into the visible realm.

So, what exactly happened when the Light manifested on the first day?

All things that were in the invisible realm were made manifest in the visible realm. If we are immersed in the Light of the New Jerusalem, if we exist in the splendor of His Light as Enoch says, we can manifest the New Jerusalem's design on the earth. In other words, we can turn on the Light switch in the darkened house and cause the Light of the Almighty to shine on the planet.

HOW WE WERE CREATED BEFORE THE FOUNDATION OF THE WORLD

This is a pioneering subject in which God wants to shed His Light to learn about Heaven's government on the Earth.

This is a pioneering subject in which God wants to shed His Light to learn about Heaven's government on the Earth.

The first thing we need to understand is where the Bible was written from? Because this is the dimension where scripture comes alive and the truths which the Author wanted to capture in it emerge. Moreover, it is the way to see things we have never seen before.

Let's begin our journey by going to the place where everything was created, wherein we will discover our nature before the world came into being.

Understanding what we are and how we were created will keep us from falling prey to the great lie of this world's system to live gloriously on the Earth.

1 | Written In The Book Of Life.

> In the beginning was the Word, and the Word was with God, and the Word was God.
>
> He was in the beginning with God. All things were made through Him, and without Him nothing was made that was made. In Him was life, and the life was the light of men.
>
> | John 1:1-4

God is Light, and one of His names is the Father of Lights[34]. We all emanate from Him as glorious lights, and before coming to Earth, we had our existence in God. Throughout the ages, every one of us, who was going to be a part of the Body of Christ was already united in Him. We were predestined for the Living Word to write Himself in us. Since then, we were already a part of the Book of Life and the families in the heavens.

> For this reason, I bow my knees to the Father of our Lord Jesus Christ, from whom every family

[34] James 1:17

> in heaven and on earth gets its name,
>
> | Ephesians 3:14-15(NIRV)

Many believe that the Book of Life is like a massive list of names, written down, that can be erased at any given moment. However, the reality is that God doesn't inscribe our names down in the Book of Life, but He **Writes Us down**. Each name is a design, a living epistle, a destiny, a function to be carried out for the complete work of Christ to manifest on the Earth.

> Nevertheless, do not rejoice in this, that the spirits are subject to you, but rather rejoice because **your names are written in heaven."**
>
> | Luke 10:20

Names are extremely important to God because they define our eternal function. Some parents, inspired by Heaven, give their children the right name. In other cases, they are utterly wrong. However, the name that God knows us by is eternal, revealing it to those who long to know it.

Jesus Christ writes to the church in Pergamos:

> To him who overcomes I will give some of the hidden manna to eat. And I will give him a white stone, and on the stone a new name written which no one knows except him who receives it.
>
> | Revelation 2:17b

He also mentions this new name when he writes to the church in Philadelphia:

> He who overcomes, I will make him a pillar in the temple of My God, and he shall go out no more. I will write on him the name of My God and the name of the city of My God, the New Jerusalem, which comes down out of heaven from My God. And I will write on him My new name.
>
> **| Revelation 3:12**

We see here how an overcomer's name is intimately connected to a heavenly identity. They were received by God's children, who, in turn, become the Temple of God and are part of the New Jerusalem. We come from Him, and we return to Him.

Valentinus, in "Gospel of Truth", says:

> The name is not mere, nor is it only terminology, but rather it is transcendental. He alone named him, he alone seeing him, he alone having the power to give him a name. Whoever does not exist has no name - for what names are given to nothings? But this existing one exists together with his name. And the father alone knows him, and he alone named him.
>
> **| Valentinus - 47 (Apocrypha)**

> Those whose names he knew first were called last, so that the one who has knowledge is one

whose name the father has pronounced. For one whose name has not been spoken is ignorant. Indeed, how shall one hear if a name has not been uttered?

Hence, whoever has knowledge is from above. If called, that person hears, replies, and turns toward him who called. That person ascends to him and knows how he is called. Having knowledge, that person does the will of him who called. That person desires to please him, finds rest, and receives a certain name. Those who thus are going to have knowledge know whence they came and whither they are going. They know it as someone who, having become intoxicated, has turned from his drunkenness and, having come to himself, has restored what is his own.

| Valentinus 12-13 Apocrypha

The Living Book is the thoughts and the Father's mind, who became flesh in Jesus Christ. He continues to reveal Himself in His Sons and Daughters, who, as little children, are filled with laughter, unconcerned about life, like babies, ever beholding their Father in Heaven without ceasing. **The Living Word lives in those who express it.**

This is acquaintance with the living book, whereby at the end he has manifested the eternal-ones as the alphabet of his revelation. These are not vowels nor are they consonants, such that someone might read them and think of emptiness, but rather they are the true alphabet by which those who recognize it are themselves ex- pressed. Each letter is a perfect thought, each letter is like a complete book written in the alphabet of unity by the Father who inscribes the eternal-ones so that thru his alphabet they might recognize the Father.

His wisdom meditates on the Meaning. His teaching expresses it. His acquaintance revealed it. His dignity is crowned by it. His joy unites with it. His glory exalted it His appearance manifested it. His repose received it His love embodied it. His faith embraced it.

Thus the Logos of the Father comes into the totality as the fruit of his heart and the face-form of his volition. But he supports them all, he atones them and moreover he assumes the face-form of everyone, purifying them, bringing them back—within the Father

| Valentinus, 15-17, Apocrypha

In Christ, we were written as a living letter before the foundation of the world. It's the letter of our design and destiny, wherein each one manifests a different aspect of Christ's fullness. When we know ourselves as we have been known, we can manifest the Living Word on the Earth. Each and every design is one of greatness, perfection, abundance, and infinite wisdom so that our temporary journey through the Earth bears fruit throughout generations.

Those who travel through life taught in everything, in abundance as in lack, in joy as in suffering, in power as in weakness, are the ones who have found their letter, and they walk in their predetermined steps. These are the ones who have found the Book of Life's fragrance and enjoy their journey, knowing that they are on their way back to the Light.

> Your eyes saw my substance, being yet unformed. And in Your book, they all were written, the days fashioned for me, when as yet there were none of them.
>
> **| Psalms 139:16**

> You number my wanderings; put my tears into Your bottle. Are they not in Your book?
>
> **| Psalms 56:8**

Moses met God face to face when he spent 40 days engulfed in His cloud of glory on Mount Sinai. I am sure that God must have allowed Him to know his heavenly self. That is why his face shone when he descended.

Moses knew so well the book of his design that he dared to challenge God to remove him from it, knowing that to do so would have meant the Father erasing the part of the Son, that was Moses in Christ. A vital chapter would have been torn out of the Book of the Living Word. Notice that Moses didn't ask Him to take him off a list but to remove him from The Book.

> Then Moses returned to the Lord and said, "Oh, these people have committed a great sin, and have made for themselves a god of gold! Yet now, if You will forgive their sin—but if not, I pray, **blot me out of Your book which You have written**." And the Lord said to Moses, "Whoever has sinned against Me, I will blot him out of My book.
>
> **| Exodus 32:31-33**

The Book of Life is also known as the Lamb's Book of Life. In other words, it's the eternal autobiography of all that God wants to make known and the way Christ manifests Himself in all those who are a part of His body.

In the other hand, those who worship the world system, is because they were never a part of this Book.

> All who dwell on the earth will worship him, whose names have not been written in the **Book of Life of the Lamb** slain from the foundation of the world.
>
> **| Revelation 13:8**

This book is in itself the Living Word, who is Himself the Life. And that Life is the light of men. Then the light that enlightens us is the book that each one of us receives with our name –not the one our parents give us, but the one the Father spoke from Heaven, our name as a Living letter of Christ's book.

2 | God Reminds Us Who We Are

When God was about to send the prophet Jeremiah, who felt like a child, unable even to speak, He talked to him about what he was before the foundation of the world. Understanding who he really was and the essence and substance from whom he had come from, would inject him with confidence to become His faithful voice on the Earth.

> Before I formed you in the womb, I knew you. Before you were born, I sanctified you. I ordained you a prophet to the nations.
>
> **| Jeremiah 1:5**

Today, God uses this same key to open our hearts so that we can have the confidence to move as true sons of Light by understanding who we really are in our heavenly identity.

> The disciples said to Jesus: "Tell us how our end will be." Jesus said: "Have you already discovered the beginning that you are now asking about the end? For where the beginning is, there the end will be too. Blessed is he who will stand at the beginning. And he will know the end, and he will not taste death."
>
> **| Thomas 18 Apocrypha**

Knowing the origin leads us to know the end of all things.

In that eternity, we lived in the dwelling place of Light. We were the sons of the day, and as such, had the authority to push darkness to its limits.

Jesus addressing His disciples, and thus, those who would believe after them, says:

> You are the light of the world. A city that is set on a hill cannot be hidden.
>
> **| Matthew 5:14**

He wasn't speaking to them as those who would one day be or become the light of the world, but as something they already were. Jesus said this before they even received the Holy Spirit.

He speaks directly to their spirit as what they were in Christ before the foundation of the world. At the same time, He tells them they are a city set on a Mount. He confirms that they were already in the heavenly city on Mount Zion, even before coming to the Earth.

Bear in mind that time does not exist in Heaven's dimensions. Therein, we were, we are (in heavenly places,) and we will be eternally.

When God spoke to Job, He asked him questions about a dimension that is not of this earth. God was speaking to his spirit, so that his eternal essence would recognize where he was created, the authority he had been granted, and what he enjoyed before he came in the flesh. Only then would he transcend every tribulation he was going through.

> Have you entered the springs of the sea? Or have you walked in search of the depths?
>
> Have the gates of death been revealed to you?
>
> Or have you seen the doors of the shadow of death?
>
> Have you comprehended the breadth of the earth?
>
> | Job 38:16-18

God did not question him to show him his weakness or ignorance, but to awaken him to God's own greatness. He needed for Job to recognize who He really was, how he was created amidst the glory and the outreach God has given him.

> Where is the way to the dwelling of light? And darkness where is its place, that you may take it to its territory, and that you may discern the paths to its home?
>
> **Do you know, because you were born then**, and the number of your days is great!
>
> | Job 38:19-21 NAS

Pain and tribulation had encapsulated Job's faith. He had lost the compass of his perfect and intimate relationship with God. This is why the Lord manifests Himself to him, to awaken his spirit to the reality of his true being.

Let us enter the dimensions of the eternal to see that ever-glorious moment that Job experienced before the world was:

The dwelling place of light and the place where darkness resides.

This is one of the accounts narrated in the "Great Melchizedek Scroll" (Apocryphal) that amplifies this passage even further without contradicting the Bible.

> Before there was a star to shine, before there were angels to sing, there was already a heaven, the home of the Eternal, the only God. Perfect in wisdom, love and glory. The Eternal One lived an eternity, before the realization of His beautiful dream, in the creation of the Universe.
>
> The innumerable beings that compose the Creation were all idealized with great love, from the tiniest particle to gigantic galaxies; everything deserving of His supreme attention. God idealized the Universe as a great orchestra that, under His rule, should vibrate harmonious chords of justice and peace. For each creature He composed a song of love.
>
> **| Melchizedek Scroll 1:1-2 Apocrypha**

In the beginning, God created the heavens and the earth, and the hosts that minister in the heavens, the cherubim, seraphim, and other angels that rule the universe. However, the hosts that would be assigned to the earth were not yet created.

3 | The Abyss Of Darkness Before Creation

> The earth hath existed waste and void, and darkness was on the face of the deep, and the Spirit of Elohim hovered on the face of the waters,
> | Genesis 1:2[35]

To better understand the state that the earth was in and what God was about to do, it is vital to note that we are talking about two different faces here: one is the "face of the deep" and the other the "face of the waters".

A face is the visible part of someone or something that others can see. A face reflects our identity and translates the features of who we are. It is the image of the invisible substance that constitutes us.

Thus, the abyss or the deep has its face, as do the waters. As we will discover both are entirely different, one from the other? Darkness was over the face of the deep, but God's Spirit was over the face of the waters. One face belongs to the kingdom of darkness and the other to the kingdom of God.

Melchizedek continues his narrative:

> As precious as life, the freedom of choice, through which creatures could demonstrate their love for the Creator, demanded a proof of fidelity. With the purpose of revealing it, the Eternal One led the hosts through the illuminated space, until he approached an abyss of darkness that contrasted

[35] Direct translation from the interlinear Hebrew.

> with the immense brightness of the galaxies. In the distance, this abyss had become insignificant to the eyes of the angels, like a dot without light; but as they approached it, it appeared in its immensity.
>
> The Creator, who at every step revealed to the angels the mysteries of His kingdom, was there in silence, as if keeping a secret for Himself. The darkness of that abyss consisted in the proof of fidelity.

| Melchizedek Scroll 1:15-16ᵃ Apocrypha

Enoch describes this same place, which he saw in one of his many trips into the heavenly dimensions.

> And I proceeded to where things were chaotic. And I saw there something horrible: I saw neither a heaven above nor a firmly founded earth, but a place chaotic and horrible. And there I saw seven stars of the heaven bound together in it, like great mountains and burning with fire.
>
> **| Enoch 21:1-3**

> For thus says the Lord God: 'When I make you a desolate city, like cities that are not inhabited, when I bring the deep upon you, and great waters cover you,
>
> then I will bring you down with those who

> descend into the Pit, to the people **of old**, and I will make you dwell **in the lowest part of the earth, in places desolate from antiquity**...
>
> | Ezekiel 26:19-20a

Isaiah is revealed how Lucifer fell before the world was, and he describes Sheol, the place of desolation where he was cast down to the lowest parts of the pit in the darkness of the deep.

> How you are fallen from heaven, O Lucifer, son of the morning!
>
> How you are cut down to the ground, you who weakened the nations![36]
>
> For you have said in your heart: 'I will ascend into heaven, I will exalt my throne above the stars of God; I will also sit on the mount of the congregation on the farthest sides of the north; I will ascend above the heights of the clouds, I will be like the Most High.' Yet you shall be brought down to **Sheol, to the lowest depths of the Pit.**
>
> | Isaiah 14: 12-15

In the Father's absolute foreknowledge, he knew of Lucifer's downfall. In the face of God's immeasurable greatness, this fallen creature was an incompetent rival that to destroy him with His sheer power would have seemed unfair. So, God devised the most incredible strategy to defeat him.

---

[36] The nations, here, refer to heavenly nations ruled by angelic princes and thrones that were weakened by Lucifer's influence and fell along with him.

Leaving his beloved city, the Lord of Light led himself in the direction of the immense abyss, about which he had been silent until then. There he stopped once more, silent as he seemed to read in the darkness a future of great struggles.

Raising his powerful arms before the darkness, he ordered in a loud voice: let there be light. Immediately the Light of his presence flooded the deep void and triumphing over the darkness revealed an unfinished world covered by crystalline waters.

With this gesture, the Eternal One began a great battle for the vindication of His government of Light; the battle of love against selfishness; of justice against injustice; of humility against pride; of freedom against bondage; of life against death.

A battle that, without truce, would extend until, in the longed-for dawn, the divine King could return victoriously to the Holy Mount Zion, where, enthroned amidst the praises of the redeemed, He would reign forever in perfect peace.

The many waters that covered that world, until then hidden, were a symbol of the eternal life that for the faithful would be conquered by the love that all sacrifices.

| Melchizedek Scroll 2:25-26 Apocrypha

4 | The Lamb That Was Slain Before The Foundation Of The World

Christ's immolation is the sacrifice of his humiliation from before the foundation of the world. As part of the divine plan, He agrees with His Father to create an earth in which He would form a new lineage of sons. It would be man, a fragile creation, susceptible to error and betrayal, an adversary far inferior to satan. This would be the great victory of the Most-High, defeating the prince of darkness by a man, the Son of God made flesh.

To create the Earth, Jesus, the Living Word, left His throne of glory and took the form of Waters of Life. Within them he created the physical water to cover the dark face of the deep. Jesus was the very "Face of the waters," the very image of God on which the Holy Spirit moved. (Genesis 1:2)

> But in taking this view they put out of their minds the memory that in the old days there was a heaven, and **an earth lifted out of the water and circled by water, by the word of God;**
>
> | 2 Peter 3:5

> **He is the image of the invisible God,** the firstborn over all creation.
>
> For **by Him all things were created** that are in heaven and that are on earth, visible and invisible, whether thrones or dominions or principalities

> or powers. All things were created through Him and for Him.
>
> And He is before all things, and **in Him all things consist**.

| Colossians 1:15-17

The Word, as the Water of Life, covered the deep, sheltered the darkness by embracing it unto Himself, absorbing it within Him, in the same way that He absorbed death, sickness, pain, and sin on the cross. He was establishing the Heavenly to then carry it out on the earthly. In this way, He immolated Himself in the heavens before the earth was formed.

The water of life and the physical water fused into one, Spirit and matter. The waters from above begat the waters below. At the same time, the waters of the deep stirred below within that unfinished world.

The Hebrew word for physical waters is the term mayim, which is also used for man's procreative waters that contain his seed.

All of creation in a fetal state within the waters, pulsated, awaiting His divine voice to give it existence.

Everything was in movement, in gestation. The noise of turbulent, agitated waters could be heard. The wind blew; it was the Spirit of God moving over the waters, brooding[37] them like a hen over her eggs, covering them, imparting the warmth of life for everything to emerge and come into being.

---

[37] The word Rachaph in the Hebrew implies a relaxed motion, and it is used in other portions of scripture to refer to how a bird broods her eggs. 7363 Strong's Concordance

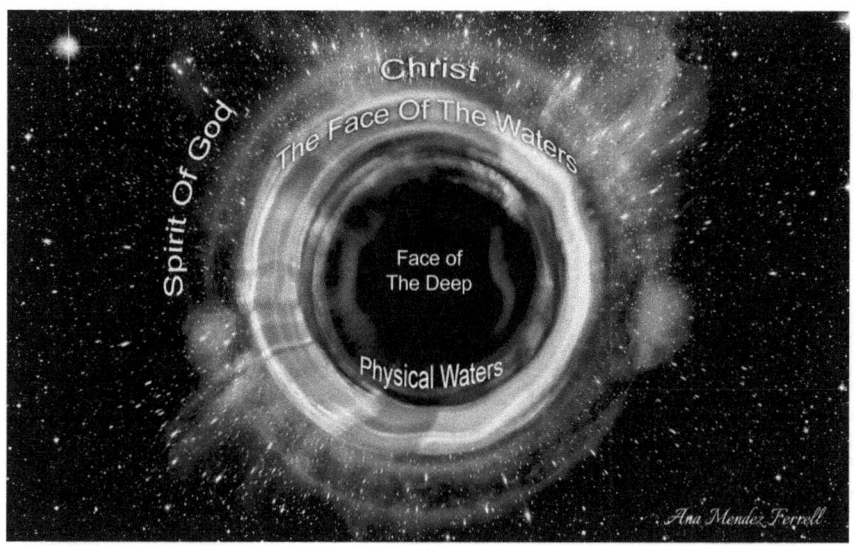

The waters above and the ones below over the face of the deep

Within those crystalline waters -waters over waters-, the primal dust, which came out of Himself, was made, so that all creation would carry His substance, His sound, and His frequency. God would be in everything created.

The dust did not come from the deep, nor the darkness, but from God Himself.

The dust in the Garden of Eden was red, from which Adam takes his name, meaning red dirt.

I personally believe that it was red because the original dust contained the blood of Jesus. The Father created man to be eternal, and only the blood of Jesus could grant him that eternal life. When Adam lost his immortal status, he also lost eternity in his blood.

Wisdom spoke:

> The Lord possessed me at the beginning of His way, before His works of old. I have been established from everlasting, from the beginning, before there was ever an earth. When there were no depths I was brought forth, when there were no fountains abounding with water.
>
> **While as yet He had not made the earth** or the fields, **or the primal dust of the world**. When He prepared the heavens, I was there, when He drew a circle on the face of the deep.

| Proverbs 8:22-24, 26-27

The Voice came from His Throne. The Father's Voice contained the Living Word that having become Light, manifested Himself in all the splendor of His glory, coming over the waters of Himself. The Father in the Son, creating all things.

> In the beginning was the Word, and the Word was with God, and the Word was God. He was in the beginning with God. All things were made through Him, and without Him nothing was made that was made. In Him was life, and the life was the light of men.

| John 1:1-4

Light and Water are the substances of the very life of Christ. The waters below, that aqueous matter, was filled with life and the creative seed that dwells in the Light.

The Darkness became agitated under the waters. It was restless, knowing that wisdom and the Father had drawn the circle of the deep, setting a limit to all its works. The hour came; the Light shone. The deep was locked up; its springs sealed. Light and Darkness were eternally separated. Job saw it from on high before the world was.

> Then God said, "Let there be a firmament in the midst of the waters, and let it divide the waters from the waters."
>
> **| Genesis 1:6**

The waters from above ascended atop the firmament, so the Waters and the Light could speak from above and form all creation. The waters below, like a mirror, reflected the countenance of Christ, who shone gloriously to give birth to the Earth. Everything, above and below, was imprinted with the face of the Son of God.

All that action was a living representation alluding to the future baptism of Jesus when He would manifest in the flesh. When the time came, the agitated Jordan perceived it; its currents stopped. The True Light, the Living Word pierced its waters, and the Spirit of God filled the Son, engulfed Him; and from above He shone like a light in the form of a dove, as the Father decreed: *This is my beloved Son in whom I am well pleased.*

The waters that separated in Genesis were united in Christ when He was immersed. The waters from above, the Life of God and the natural waters. The Son would make all things new.

Jesus is the image of the Living God. The image[38]. that, just like a seal on wet clay, was to shape all of creation to reflect His image.

The waters below were impregnated with the primal dust, which, charged with all of God's creative power, began to settle in the depths, to gloriously emerge at the sound of the Word of God who gathering all the waters under the heavens in one place, commanded: Let the dry land be uncovered!

And the land emerged like a bed of crops in a greenhouse. From it, the children of Light of every generation pulsated, each one awaiting their time to be born.

5 | Sons Of The Day

The sons of the Day are the sons of faith that God promised Abraham.

> Blessing I will bless you and multiplying I will multiply your descendants as the stars of the heaven and as the sand which is on the seashore; and your descendants shall possess the gate of their enemies.
> **| Genesis 22:17**

This word speaks to us far beyond multitudes, encapsulating within itself the divine and heavenly traits of the Sons of God.

---

[38] - The word in the Greek to define Christ as the image of the invisible God is Character which is the tool or mold used for an impression.

There are many things on earth that can represent multitudes. For example, God could have said, as the dust of the earth or the leaves on the trees, but He specifically chose as the stars from the Heaven and the sand by the sea.

I will talk about the stars in our next chapter. But I would like you to notice here that God gives Abraham this word on Mount Moriah, in the middle of Jerusalem, in an entirely arid desert, far from the sea.

It is very possible that Abraham may have never seen the sea –all of his journeys and battles took place in regions far from the coastlines. Even the Dead Sea didn't exist back then since it was formed on the ruins of Sodom and Gomorrah. So why didn't God tell him that his children would be like the sand of the desert that was a territory with which he was well acquainted?

Abraham had to see something by faith because he was going to be made the father of faith.

As I meditated on this one sunrise, at the beach, a light came to me, allowing me to see what God had told the patriarch.

There are two types of sand on the beach: a dry one, which remains untouched by the water, and a wet one, continually washed by the waves. As the Sun began to rise, Heaven was flooded with the dawn's golden majesty. The Sun's rays mirrored off the waves of the sea like liquid gold. It was then that I saw the hidden mystery in God's promise to Abraham. The sand continually washed in the waters of the sea, extended out like a mirror reflecting the glory of Heaven.

Such are the Sons of Light, continually soaked in the waters of His Presence, whose lives are the mirror of God's Glory. They are the open scroll of the Word of Life for the world to read.

The living epistles of God, the letters of light with which Heaven speaks and sings the most sublime worship to the Father, declares His oracles and pours out His wisdom into them.

Every son is a star shining in the firmament, a living letter penned by the Hand of God, announcing His handiwork.

> The heavens declare the glory of God, and the firmament shows His handiwork.
>
> Day unto day utters speech, and night unto night reveals knowledge.
>
> There is no speech nor language where their voice is not heard.
>
> **| Psalms 19:1-3**

The firmament is the book of life displayed from infinity to infinity, where every star, every gleaming Son, announces the work of His hands—no language, no words, but by merely being a genuine son of the Most High.

Chapter 6

THE RAQIA

We will now enter an exciting level of understanding in this chapter designed to lead us to know our governmental role in the heavens and our design to be light here on earth.

As I said in the previous chapter, it is vital to understand that the Bible was not written through human reasoning. The Word of Life comes from Heaven and its language, in many cases, is heavenly in nature.

> And He said to them, "You are from beneath; **I am from above**. You are of this world; **I am not of this world**.

> He went on to say in this same exchange with the Jews:
>
> Why do you not understand My speech? Because you are not able to listen to My word.
>
> | **John 8:23 & 43**

Jesus was not referring to the Hebrew language, but to the spiritual language with which He shared the Father's mysteries.

There are things He said that only those who are His disciples can understand –just as He intended it to be.

> And He said, *"To you it has been given to know the mysteries of the kingdom of God, but to the rest it is given in parables, that 'Seeing they may not see, and hearing they may not understand.'"*
>
> | **Luke 8:10**

With this clear, we will now try to unveil one of these wonderful mysteries, which is the firmament, God's RAQIA.

> In the beginning God created the heavens and the earth.
>
> | **Genesis 1:1**

The Hebrew word for "heavens" is written in the plural; it's the term Shamayim meaning the set of all the heavens.

Within the *Shamayim*, there are several levels, dimensions, or heavens. For example, Paul mentions about having been taken into the third heaven.

We find one of these heavenly levels or spaces in the first chapter of Genesis verse six, where we come across another interesting word.

> Then God said, "Let there be a **firmament** in the midst of the waters, and let it divide the waters from the waters."
>
> | Genesis 1:6

The word **"firmament"** in the English language is the Hebrew word for **Raqia**[39].

We see a more explicit description of the Raqia on the fourth day of Creation, where we find an account of how God is to use it.

> Then God said, "Let there be lights in the firmament of the heavens to divide the day from the night; and let them be for signs and seasons, and for days and years;
>
> | Genesis 1:14

---

[39] - raqia: **The heavenly vault**, or 'firmament,' Genesis 1:6,7 (3 t. in verse); Genesis 1:8 (called שָׁמַיִם; all P), Psalm 19:2 ('"" זֹהַר הָר'), הַשָּׁמַיִם Daniel 12:3; also רְ הַשָּׁמָיִם' Genesis 1:14,15,17, הָשׁ 'עַלפְּנֵי ר' Genesis 1:20

Shamayim Raqia

If I read it at first sight with my natural mind, I might quickly think that it refers to the sun, moon, and stars, visible to the natural eye. However, what it says in the original Hebrew is: Let there be luminaries in the Raqia of the Shamayim. In other words, let there be a firmament amid the heavens.

This firmament made up of these lights is much more than just the sun, moon, and stars that we see. Most of us have read Genesis and know that the earth was made in six days. But when we look at Genesis chapter 2, we find something amazing:

> Thus, the heavens and the earth, and all the host of them, were finished.
>
> | Genesis 2:1

So, the question here is on which of the six days were the hosts (armies) of heaven and earth created? Notice that he's talking about hosts that exist in both realms –the heavenly and the earthly.

These were made on the fourth day when God created the Raqia.

So, let's not just think about the stars rationally, but let us project ourselves to understand these heavenly beings, the armies created and set by the Lord amid this firmament, otherwise known as the Raqia.

We read that these luminaries, these spiritual beings, were placed to separate the Day from the night.

1 | Day And Night

When you read Genesis, it's important to note that each Day of creation doesn't refer to a day and a night like ours, because the author writes that the evening and the morning were one Day.

This word evening[40] is different from the word night, because the latter refers to the kingdom of darkness.

---

[40] Evening was considered the moment at dusk before nightfall.

That's why when the Light of the First Day is released, the first thing God does is to separate the Day from the night, that is, the realm of Light from the realm of darkness – both referring to spiritual places.

Throughout the Bible, we will see how these are used to identify the Sons of the Day and the sons of night.

Both of these two dimensions are completely different from the concept of the evening and morning, which denote natural physical days at the time of creation.

Now coming back to the fourth day, it says that these luminaries were established to separate the Day from the night. So, they are actually angelical beings with the authority to separate these two realms. This has to do with a specific class of angels that are going to minister together with the sons of God.

This is precisely what the angel of the Lord tells John while he was caught up in heaven in the book of Revelation:

> ***I am your fellow servant,*** and of your brethren who have the testimony of Jesus.
>
> **| Revelation 19:10**

A fellow servant is not one who serves someone else but rather collaborates with another of his or her same rank. They have the same mission and work alongside each other –one in heaven and the other on earth.

In this same way, the luminaries are set to operate in unity with the sons of God.

And let them be for lights in the firmament of the heavens (in the Raqia of the Shamayim) to give light on the earth"; and it was so.

Then God made two great lights: the greater light to rule the day, and the lesser light to rule the night. He made the stars also.

God set them in the Raqia of the Shamayim (firmament of the heavens) to give light on the earth,

and to **rule** over the day and over the night, and to divide the light from the darkness. And God saw that it was good. So the evening and the morning were the fourth day.

| **Genesis 1:15-19**

Here, we see that these lights are designed to execute a governmental role, which is to **rule**, indicating an intelligent verb and not just merely a shining star that provides us with heat and Light. Its purpose is to separate the Light from the darkness.

This Raqia is where the armies of God operate. There we find this angelic order called "luminaries" and also the stars that exist therein. Among the latter, there are different angels of different ranks, as well as human beings.

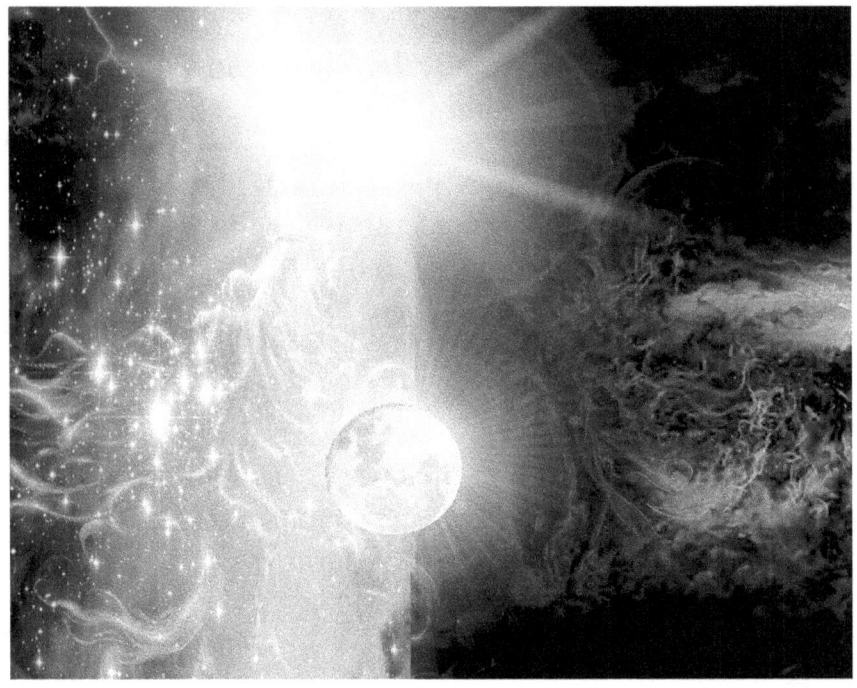

The luminaries rule, separating the day from the night

Enoch, who was given in-depth knowledge about these luminaries, writes about this segment:

> And after that I saw the hidden and the visible path of the moon, and she accomplishes the course of her path in that place by day and by night-the one holding a position opposite to the other (sun and moon) before the Lord of Spirits. And they give thanks and praise and rest not; for unto them is their thanksgiving rest.
>
> For the sun changes for a blessing or a curse, and the course of the path of the moon is light to the righteous and darkness to the sinners in

> the name of the Lord, who made a separation between the light and the darkness, and divided the spirits of men, and strengthened the spirits of the righteous, in the name of His righteousness.

| Enoch 41:7-8 (Book of Parables)

What do I mean by human beings in the Raqia?

When we were created before the foundation of the world, the first thing God did was put our star in the firmament, which was a part of the invisible world at that time. We were beings of light in the Kingdom of God. The Word of God says that the Father has blessed us with every spiritual blessing in the heavenly places in Christ, just as He chose us in Him before the foundation of the world...[41].

My star in the firmament

[41] - Ephesians 1:3-4

These heavenly places are God's Raqia, which belongs to both dimensions: first, the invisible one, and after the fourth day, to the visible one.

When God made Adam, his star began to shine in the Raqia because he was created to rule through the Kingdom of Light. We are the Light of the world, and this is not just a concept but a deep spiritual understanding, as we have already seen.

When God separates the Light from darkness on the first day, a space, a division was created between the two. This is where He places the Raqia, after separating the waters above from the waters below.

I found an interesting passage in the Hebrew version of the Book of Enoch. There are three books by Enoch, and I'm citing the third one.

What struck me upon reading it was the translator's use of the word "Raqia:"

> When the holy one, blessed be he, went out and went in: from the garden of Eden, and from Eden to the garden, from the garden to Raqia and from Raqia to the garden of Eden, then all and everyone beheld the splendor of His Shekina[42], and they were not injured until the generations of Enoch, who was the chief of all the worshipers in the world.
>
> **| Hebrew Book of Enoch 5**

When Enoch was translated to heavenly places, even the angels wondered what he was doing there.

[42] Hebrew word for Glory

Elohim[43] went in and out of the Raqia, into the garden of Eden

The point I am wanting to make is that the Garden of Eden was linked to the Raqia. It was the point of connection for God to move through the physical and heavenly realms in the Garden of Eden.

The Garden of Eden was not entirely physical, but it was bidimensional. The heavens and the earth gathered therein. That is why Adam and his wife could eat from the fruit trees and the Tree of Life, and unfortunately also from the tree of the knowledge of good and evil. They could see God's Holy Mount and the Father walked with them. They could hear God's Voice in the soft evening breeze, when the Raqia was visible and they were clothed in robes of light.

> When the cool evening breezes were blowing, the man and his wife heard the Lord God walking

[43] One of God's names

> about in the garden.
>
> **| Genesis 3:8a**[44]

The two dimensions, united, were indeed a beautiful and amazing sight to behold. However, the only way that Adam and his wife could see the stars was in their heavenly nature, the beautiful shiny luminaries performing their duties from above. Remember there was no night in paradise, just evening. And stars cannot be seen in the evening if they were only from the physical dimension.

On the other hand, before it ever rained on the earth in Noah's time, a mist covered the entire planet; thus, it was impossible to see the moon and stars, and probably not even the sun.

> For the Lord God had not caused it to rain on the earth, and there was no man to till the ground; but a mist went up from the earth and watered the whole face of the ground.
>
> **| Genesis 2:5b-6**

If the luminaries were placed as signs for seasons, days, and years, and to illuminate the Earth, then they needed to be seen. This was only possible in the Garden of Eden by beholding the heavenly dimension and the luminaries as the hosts in the Raqia.

Today we see, with our natural eyes, the result of a fallen firmament, but behind it lies the true one that marks the seasons of God for man. It is where the children of Light can hear the Father's appointed times, decreeing them in unison with the Spirit, upon the Earth.

---

[44] -. New Living Translation

Now, Jesus came to restore what was lost; that is, the Garden of Eden joined to the Raqia.

However, the problem is that due to man's fall, night covered the Earth, and the devil set up for himself a false Raqia. That is why, when Adam and his wife were removed from the garden, satan incited human beings to worship the sun, moon, and stars, because he knew the luminaries were needed to govern the Earth.

The first night and the false raqia

The third book of Enoch describes how these luminaries were seized and forced to serve satan's government.

> What did the generation of Enoch do? They went from one end of the World to the other, and each one brought silver, gold, precious stones, and pearls in huge heaps like mountains and

> heels. They made idols out of them throughout the whole world. They erected the idols in every quarter of the world. The size of each item was 1000 parasangs. They brought down the sun, the moon, planets and constellations, placed them before the idols on the right hand and on their left, to attend them just as they attend the sacred one -may he be blessed! As it is written (1 Kings 22:19), "all of the armies of heaven were standing next to him on his right hand and on his left".
>
> What power did they have that they were able to bring them down? They would not have been able to bring them down, but for Uzza, Azza and Azazel who taught them sorceress, by which means they brought them down and made use of them.
>
> **| Hebrew book of Enoch 5** [45]

In this reading, it is evident that the sun, moon, and stars were not the bodies of stars that we see shining in the firmament today, but rather spiritual beings that could be arrested and brought down to feed their idolatry.

This is why our understanding of the Raqia plays such an important role. Because God's government has to do with luminaries joined together with the Son of God.

We see a very interesting portion of scripture in the book of Judges, in which Sisera's army used the stars to conquer in battle.

---

[45] Third Book of Enoch, new Hebrew translation, chapter 1, page 175. Complete books of Enoc, Dr A. Nyland

> From the heavens the stars fought, from their courses they fought with Sisera.
>
> | **Judges 5:20 Interlineal Bible**[46]

2 | Heavenly Body

Although luminaries are spiritual beings, we, as God's children, are also stars and have a celestial body. In our manifestation as light, united with our star and in collaboration with the luminaries, we have the power to tear down the false Raqia.

We are the light and have the power to tear down the false Raqia

Let's take a look at this Biblically. When the Apostle Paul talks about our spiritual body, he is careful in using this precise term. However, in this portion of scripture, he uses a different word, referring to us not only as an earthly and spiritual body but as a "celestial body," as well.

[46] The Interlineal Bible uses the word IM that means "with" Strong concordance 5973 Other translations wrongly use against Sisera

> There are also celestial bodies and terrestrial bodies; but the glory of the celestial is one, and the glory of the terrestrial is another.
>
> **| 1 Corinthians 15:40**

If we read this with our natural mind, we might believe that it refers to the level of brightness we will one day have in our resurrected bodies after death. But this is something much deeper that we need to understand. Paul isn't talking about our level of brightness once we leave the earth, but about our celestial body in the resurrection, while still alive.

He establishes that in addition to having a spiritual body, we also have a celestial one. This means that we have a natural physical body, a spiritual one – our spirit within us– but we also have a celestial body seated with Christ in heavenly places. Our spirit is connected to our heavenly being, and it operates in the power of our celestial body.

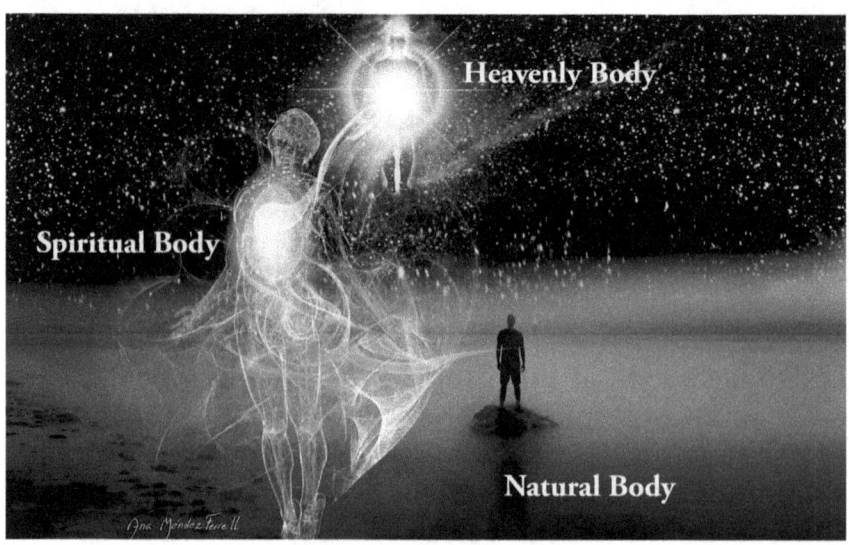

Heavenly Body, Spiritual Body, Natural Body

Allow me to explain this further.

Paul goes on to say in this same epistle, that as is the earthly man, so are those of earth, and as is the heavenly man, so also are those who are of heaven. (verse 48)

Notice that Paul is talking about Jesus Christ as a heavenly being.

He is not saying: As is the earthly, so are those of earth, and as is the spiritual so are those of the Spirit.

What I want you to understand is that there is a celestial body that exists over each and every one of us. It is our being before the foundation of the world, which is made visible to our natural eye as a star in the firmament.

As is the heavenly man, so also are those who are of heaven.

We see this because the first thing the wise men saw when Jesus was born on the earth was His star shining in the sky.

The writers of the Bible often use the names of stars to represent the person of Jesus Christ, such as the Sun of Righteousness, or the Bright and Morning Star.

Peter puts it this way:

> And so, we have the prophetic word confirmed, which you do well to heed as a light that shines in a dark place, until the day dawns and the Morning Star rises in your hearts.
>
> **| 2 Peter 1:19**

My star over me

The Book of Ezekiel also mentions this Raqia when he sees the living creatures.

> Now stretched over the heads of the living beings there was something like an expanse, looking like the terrible and awesome shimmer of icy crystal.
>
> **| Ezekiel 1:22**

This word "expanse" is the term "Raqia."

So, we see a Raqia over these living creatures, just like there is one over us today. These move by wheels that turn around themselves.[47]

> Now over the heads of the living beings there was something like **an expanse** (Raqia,) like the awesome gleam of crystal, spread out over their heads.
>
> | Ezekiel 1:26

The Raqia above the heads of the living creatures is what connects them directly to the authority of the Throne.

In the following illustration, we see the living creatures and God's Throne dimension, together with the Raqia over them.

The four living creatures and the Raqia and God's throne

---

[47] In my book "The Spirit of man" I explain in great extend the wheels of our spirit.

As we too are stars within the Raqia, we are directly illuminated by God's Throne to understand His perfect will and be led by Him. This is where our celestial being immersed in Christ connects us to the Throne of His Government.

While Ezekiel observed the Raqia over the living creatures' heads as a beautiful gleam of crystal under the Throne, John saw the exact same vision from the Throne.

> Before the throne there was a sea of glass, like crystal. And in the midst of the throne, and around the throne, were four living creatures full of eyes in front and in back.
>
> **| Revelation 4:6**

Both of them saw the Waters above, which is Christ, wrapping the Raqia's firmament within Himself.

3 | The Raqia And The Heavenly City

I want to link this subject of the Raqia to the New Jerusalem, which we discussed earlier. We saw how the New Jerusalem is our state of resurrection and the city where we dwell as sons of God. The city is in us, and we are in the city. We also saw that by entering the City is how our heavenly habitation could be formed within us. This transformation first begins in our celestial being and then is transmitted to our spiritual being.

Notice that I am marking a clear difference between our spiritual being and our celestial being.

In the second epistle to the Corinthians, the Apostle Paul once again mentions this celestial nature.

The New Jerusalem covering our celestial being

> For indeed in this body we groan, longing to be clothed with our [immortal, eternal] celestial body,
>
> | **2 Corinthians 5:2 (Amp)**

The resurrection is our foundation in Christ, which indwells and quickens **our spirit**, imbuing it with immortal life. But the Light by which we shine in perpetuity comes from God's Raqia over us, that is, from the throne to which it is connected.

To the degree that we merge with the Father and the Son and are clothed in His Holiness, love, and righteousness will determine how bright our star shines.

Concerning this brightness, Enoch writes:

> And I saw other lightnings and the **stars of heaven**, and I saw how He called them **all by their names** and they hearkened unto Him.
>
> And I saw how they are weighed in a righteous balance according to their proportions of light: (I saw) the width of their spaces and the day of their appearing, and how their revolution produces lightning: and (I saw) their revolution according to the number of the angels, and (how) they keep faith with each other.
>
> And I asked the angel who went with me who showed me what was hidden: 'What are these?' And he said to me: 'The Lord of Spirits hath showed thee their his parable: **these are the names of the holy who dwell on the earth** and believe in the name of the Lord of Spirits for ever and ever.
>
> | Enoch 43:1-4[48]

We previously spoke of how the resurrection and the New Jerusalem are united and are, in some way, the same essence. It is because of the resurrection that I am born into the Heavenly City.

[48] Complete Book of Enoch, By Dr. A. Nyland pg 49

In Isaiah's splendid description of the New Jerusalem, we see the appearance of these luminaries again.

> The sun shall no longer be your light by day, nor for brightness shall the moon give light to you; but the Lord will be to you an everlasting light, and your God your glory.
>
> **| Isaiah 60:19**

Here, it clearly refers to the stars that light up the earth in a natural way.

Now I would like you to notice that between verses 19 and 20, Isaiah marks a difference between the physical sun and moon and the heavenly ones.

We just read that the sun and moon will no longer be our lights. But notice the way it is written in verse 20 using the pronoun "Your" before these lights:

> **Your sun** shall no longer go down, nor shall **your moon** withdraw itself; For the Lord will be your everlasting light, and the days of your mourning shall be ended.
>
> **| Isaiah 60:20**

Here, we see exactly the same thing that the Apostle Paul mentioned in his epistle to the Corinthians. We have a celestial body that will give us light and illuminate our life.

Thus, in the natural world we move by the light of the sun –*as is the earthly, so are those who are of the earth.*

But in the spiritual realm, Jesus is our Light illuminating us from the Raqia.

In our fallen earthly nature, we are separated from Christ. Then we come to the Lord and align to our heavenly nature in the spiritual world.

My star rules in the Raqia, but it is subject to and illuminated by the Sun of Righteousness.

We are all one same firmament, each with its place from where we shine. No star stands in the way of another, and all are beautiful. When Christ, the Sun of Righteousness rises, the stars fade away. They continue to shine, but you can no longer see them because the Son becomes the only visible radiance. We are absorbed in His Light, and the world sees only Him.

Immersed in Christ, our Greatest Light

This is where the new birth takes on a much deeper construct than the religious theory we have been taught.

When I am born of the Water and the Spirit, I begin to move in my heavenly nature.

When I am born again in my heavenly being

Now let us compare Isaiah's passage, where it speaks of our sun and moon no longer going down, with John's vision of the Holy City.

> But I saw no temple in it, for the Lord God Almighty and the Lamb are its temple. The city had no need of the sun or of the moon to shine in it, for the glory of God illuminated it. The Lamb is its light
>
> **| Revelation 21:22-23**

We see here how our heavenly nature consists of Christ having completely absorbed us into Himself. We don't cease to exist but remain as stars within Him. That celestial body, clothed with the Sun of Righteousness, becomes the nature through which we can govern with Him, as one same spirit and mind, in complete oneness.

The luminaries were set to rule. And only when I am truly born again of the Water, which is Christ and His Spirit, can I connect with my heavenly nature. This will result in my no longer seeing myself as an earthly, mortal being but as a luminary called to be a light unto the world.

> I swear to you, you righteous, that in Heaven the Angels remember you for good in front of the Glory of the Great One, and that your names are written down in front of the Glory of the Great One. Be hopeful! For you were formerly put to shame through evils and afflictions, but now **you will shine like the Lights of Heaven, and will be seen**, and the Gate of Heaven will be opened to you.
>
> **| Enoch 104:1-2**

Let us recall what I started to share about the living creatures and how they have a Raqia above their head, connected to the Throne of God. This is precisely what happens to us once we are inside the New Jerusalem. We are clothed in our celestial habitation. The Raqia and the Light, which is Christ, are above us, as well as the Throne of God. This is how we become the temple of the Living God.

> For the signs and the times and the years and the days the angel Uriel showed to me, whom

> the Lord of glory hath set for ever over **all the luminaries of the heaven, in the heaven and in the world, that they should rule on the face of the heaven and be seen on the earth,**
>
> and be leaders for the day and the night, i.e. the sun, moon, and stars, and all the **ministering creatures which make their revolution in all the chariots of the heaven**.
>
> **| Enoch 75:3**

These ministering creatures, which make their revolution in the chariots of heaven, could very well be the living creatures that Ezekiel saw, or perhaps another angelic order, after the order of the luminaries.

4 | Light Bearers

What we have in common as sons of God with the luminaries is that we are both bearers of God's Light. The Hebrew word for "Luminary" is *Maor*, which means "Carrier of the heavenly Light".

Now, there's something very interesting in this regard in the book of Proverbs.

> The light of the eyes rejoices the heart…
>
> **| Proverbs 15:30a**

The word used for light in the eyes in this verse, is once again the term *Maor*.

This means that once we are clothed in the New Jerusalem, reunited with our celestial being, our star shines within us, and its light can be seen through our eyes.

Obviously, not like laser beams as we see in science fiction movies, but as a spiritual glimmer that others can easily perceive.

This is why it is also written that a peaceful heart makes others joyful. Because this is the place where God's Light emanates from; the Light of the first day, which is perceived by others as joy, righteousness and peace. They can't explain it. They don't know what it is. It's not something that can be seen with our natural eyes, but the spirit in people around us can feel it.

> As is the earthly man, so are those who are of the earth; and as is the heavenly man, so also are those who are of heaven.
>
> **| 1 Corinthians 15:48**

His gleaming light radiates over all the earth. The resplendence of His Raqia shines upon all those who seek Him, making Himself visible and palpable.

> His disciples said: "Show us the place where you are, because it is necessary for us to seek it. He said to them: "Whoever has ears should hear! Light exists inside a person of light, and he shines on the whole world. If he does not shine, there is darkness."
>
> **| Thomas 23**

There's a generation of sons of light rising up, those who have ears to hear and eyes to see. And this is the glorious freedom of the sons of God that is to be manifested. All will receive the impact and the fruit thereof. They are tearing down the false Raqia. In many places, the air feels lighter. Some will probably just feel that there's something new in the atmosphere. But others will understand, and a new brightness will be born within them.

> "Jesus says:
>
> Let the one who seeks continue seeking until he finds what he is looking for. And when he finds it, he will become troubled. And when he is dismayed, when he becomes troubled, he will be amazed. And he will rule over the All," and he will find rest.
>
> **| Thomas 2 Apocrypha[49]**

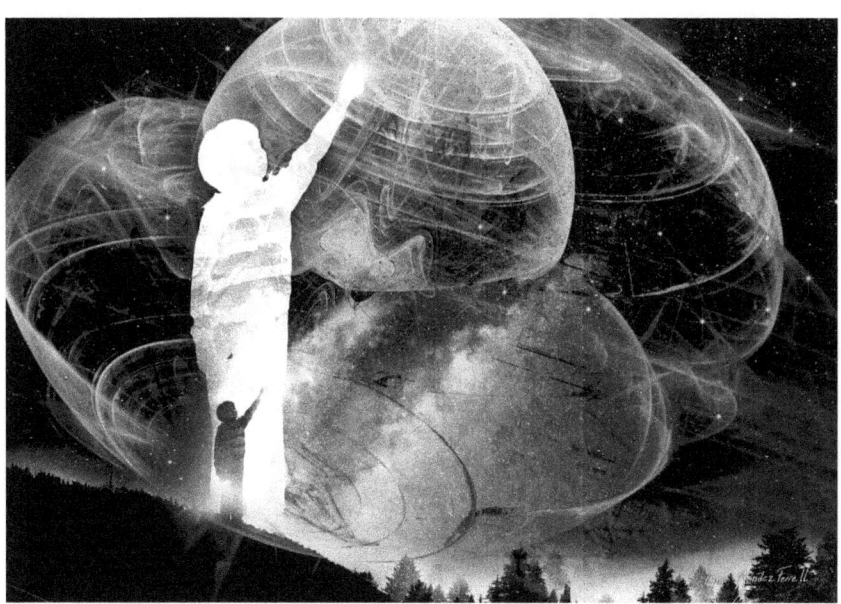

My Heavenly me

[49] I put together the Coptic and the Greek translation so we can get its fullness. The Greek adds: and he will find rest. While the Coptic omits this last sentence.

Chapter 7

CONNECTING TO OUR CELESTIAL BEING

1 | Heavenly Birth

Being born of the Water and of the Spirit are perhaps some of the tritest words in the Church today, yet they deserve a deep review in the light of a new day emerging.

My level of authority and knowledge of the Kingdom of God are intimately linked to my understanding of my heavenly nature.

Unless I am born of the Water and the Spirit, I will never connect with my celestial being.

The Cross is the path that sanctifies and transforms us. It is where we find the Blood and the Water that make up the living waters of Christ. We immerse in them to activate this metamorphosis and reconnect to our heavenly nature.

> Jesus says: "If the flesh came into being because of the spirit, it is a wonder. But if the spirit (came into being) because of the body, it is a wonder of wonders. Yet I marvel at how this great wealth has taken up residence in this poverty."
>
> | **Thomas 29 Apocrypha**

The Spirit of God created the flesh. But the wonder is how God, by His Spirit can bring forth, out of our fallen flesh a new creation. This was only possible when Christ, through His sacrifice, died to the flesh, to give birth to the Sons of God, by the Spirit.

This is why the new birth is intimately connected to our resurrected state in Christ, which is also the light and life of my celestial being.

> If then you were raised with Christ, seek those things which are above, where Christ is, sitting at the right hand of God.
>
> | **Colossians 3:1**

That is, seated in the heavenly city, where He is the King of Salem and High Priest according to the order of Melchizedek.

> Set your mind on things above, not on things on the earth. For you died, and your life is hidden with Christ in God.
>
> **| Colossians 3:2-3**

I die to my earthly nature by entering the waters of baptism, but it is the waters of the Cross that transform me. **I must allow the Cross to shape me, so His divine nature fuses with mine.**

> When Christ who is our life appears, then you also will appear with Him in glory.
>
> **|Colossians 3:4**

Paul is not talking, here, about a future global manifestation of Christ, but when He manifests Himself in the life of every one of us. Peter alludes to this same mater when he says: until the Morning Star rises in your hearts.[50]

When this takes place, we manifest with Him in glory, shining with the Light of God, both in heaven and on earth. Then our nature is absorbed in His glory so that we can manifest His Light.

This genuine birth of the Water and the Spirit has to do with our glorification.

> Moreover, whom He predestined, these He also called; whom He called, these He also justified; and whom He justified, **these He also glorified.**
>
> **| Romans 8:30**

[50] 2 Peter 1:19

> **And the glory which You gave Me I have given them,** that they may be one just as We are one.
>
> | John 17:22

Our celestial being has already been glorified, and now we must make that connection with our body in glory while still alive, here, on Earth.

I am physically on the earth, but Ana also has a celestial body in Heaven.

We see this when Jesus talks to Nicodemus about the new birth. After introducing him to the concept of a spiritual birth versus a natural birth, Christ explains that there are earthly things, and there are heavenly things.

> If I have told you earthly things and you do not believe, how will you believe if I tell you heavenly things? **No one has ascended to heaven** but He who came down from heaven, that is, **the Son of Man who is in heaven.**
>
> | John 3:12-13

Here, we see how Jesus being on earth, speaks of Himself as someone who has ascended to Heaven and is in heaven. He said this long before the Ascension, leading us to understand how in the spirit, we have the power to ascend into heaven and be there, while still here on Earth. We were predestined to be made according to the image of the Son.

Likewise, when we are born again and absorbed into

Christ, in the New Jerusalem, we are here on earth, but we are also in Heaven.

My being in Jesus and Jesus in the New Jerusalem

Jesus once again introduces the subject of the waters of life when he explains about the rivers of living water that will flow from within those who believe in Him.

> But this He spoke concerning the Spirit, whom those believing in Him would receive; for the Holy Spirit was not yet given, because Jesus was not yet glorified.
>
> **| John 7:39**

So, after the resurrection, Jesus ascended into the heavens to be glorified and send the Holy Spirit to the Earth. And it is in Him that we can be clothed in our heavenly habitation, to fulfill the scripture that says: *as is the heavenly Man, so also are those who are heavenly.*[51]

This is why receiving the infilling of the Holy Spirit, goes beyond just speaking in tongues or having the Gifts of the Spirit.

The utmost that Jesus longed for was His glorification because only then would He be able to beget the Sons of God, according to His image, and dwell in them.

As the King of Kings reigning over the Earth, Jesus Christ needed a governmental body, composed of His angels and His Saints, to rule with Him. After sitting on the throne, He unifies the Heavens and the Earth and opens up the possibility of reconnecting us with our heavenly being, which is who we were before the foundation of the world. This is how we are positioned as stars in God's Raqia, which was His original design: to reign with Him.

2 | We Were Predestined

> For whom He foreknew, He also **predestined to be conformed to the image of His Son**, that He might be the firstborn among many brethren.
>
> | Romans 8:29

We began to touch on the subject of our celestial being by introducing the subject of the Raqia. We also studied how

---

[51] - 1 Corinthians 15:48

God blessed us in heavenly places before the foundation of the world. Now we are seeing that we were predestined to be made according to the image of Christ.

When we think of the word predestination, we may believe that there's a whole design, similar to a map of things, per se, that need to happen to us in life and that we were predestined to live them out. This misconception of predestination caused several 16th. Century reformers to reject this idea.

This passage in the book of Romans talks about something that took place before the foundation of the world. We were predestined to have the image of the Son of God throughout eternity.

So, this concept of predestination actually refers to how we were created in God and in the heavens.

Let's see what Paul, himself, said to the Corinthians:

> But we speak the wisdom of God in a mystery, hidden wisdom which God ordained before the ages for our glory
>
> **| 1 Corinthians 2:7**

Here we see that there is a wisdom imparted to us before God created all things, which is hidden from the eyes of the world and has to do with our glorification.

As I said earlier, being filled with His Spirit is our becoming one with our heavenly being.

3 | The Two Personas

According to the dictionary, the word "persona" is defined as the *individual substance* of a rational nature. This is a term mostly used in psychology. This comes from the fact that, in modern times, human beings were made the center of the rational universe. Kant, a philosopher, describes this as a man's personality, which is an end in itself.

From an early childhood, a structure of thought patterns and behavior is formed within us. And throughout our life, it becomes the subconscious program that manages 95% of our actions and reactions.[52]

This is the foundational structure of who I am in this world. I'm going to call this **"the persona I created"**. It will have its own way of navigating life, its own culture, and its own worldview. The important thing here is that I am the one who created this persona, and it's completely opposite to the person that God created me to be.

The persona that I formed was made according to the reality of the world around me, and the person created by God, was formed according to His wisdom before the foundation of the world.

The soul is responsible for the creation and operation of "my self-created persona." The soul is not the persona, but it nurtures it and causes it to function. It is also the link connecting my body to my spirit.[53]

---

[52] From Emerson Ferrell's class series "Remembering Our Future" at www.voiceofthelight.com

[53] In my book The Spirit of Man, I describe at length all of the functions of the soul and the spirit.

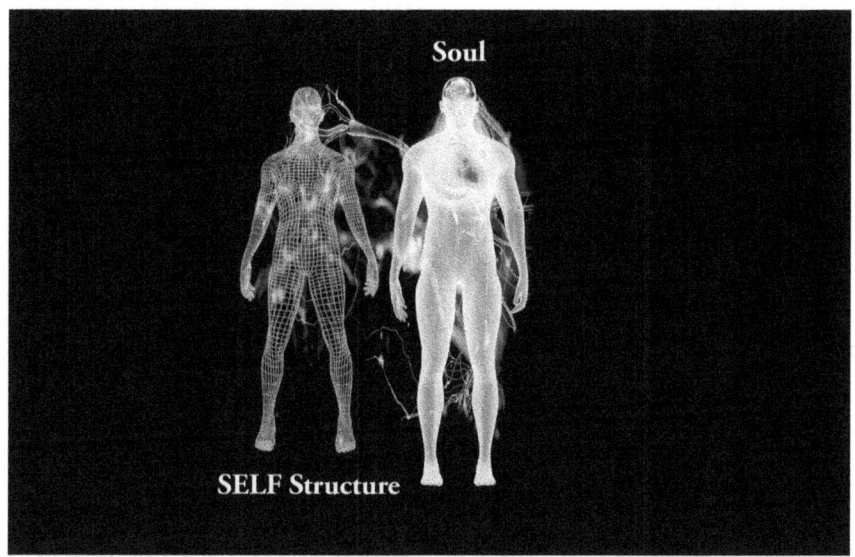

For a moment, let's imagine an example of that persona created by one of us. This persona was formed in the chaos of a dysfunctional family, leading to a personality riddled with rejection, inferiority complexes, and fear of many things. Moreover, she always feels threatened by the fear of illness and death. A series of insecurities were also formed in her, coupled with man's fear and expressing what she feels.

All of this, or whatever each one has created, becomes a structure or edifice, per se, which ends up becoming the foundation or structure of our SELF.

This structure becomes the guide for how I move, work, and react here on earth.

These frameworks start to be in force from the moment of the fall. But God created us to be in the image of the Son of God.

When Adam was created, he functioned according to his heavenly persona or heavenly self. God had formed this personality or this perfect persona for man to operate through and be of great power and wisdom upon the earth.

When man ate the fruit of the tree of the knowledge of good and evil, he separated from his celestial self and started creating his own persona.

So, once again, the soul is the instrument, the engine, the mechanism allowing our self-created persona, to function and have life in itself.

On the other hand, our spirit is comprised of all the organs and functions our celestial body needs to become visible and operate through us. **Our spirit is not our heavenly being, but the spiritual organism designed to manifest it.**

When the Bible calls us to put our old creature to death, it is talking about destroying that structure we created. Our soul isn't what has to die. And when we put all that corrupt creation to death, our soul does not die, we continue to have our mind, our will, and our emotions.

I want to clarify that there is a big difference between the soul, with all its functions, and "the persona" you and I created. That persona or personality is the one that I need to place on the cross. My soul remains to serve the "new creation". The soul once subject to my spirit will transmit the thoughts and power of my celestial being.

In the following image, we see the two personas: the structure created by our soul and our heavenly self-created by God. The persona in corruption is connected to the soul who created it and makes it work. And the heavenly self is connected to our spirit.

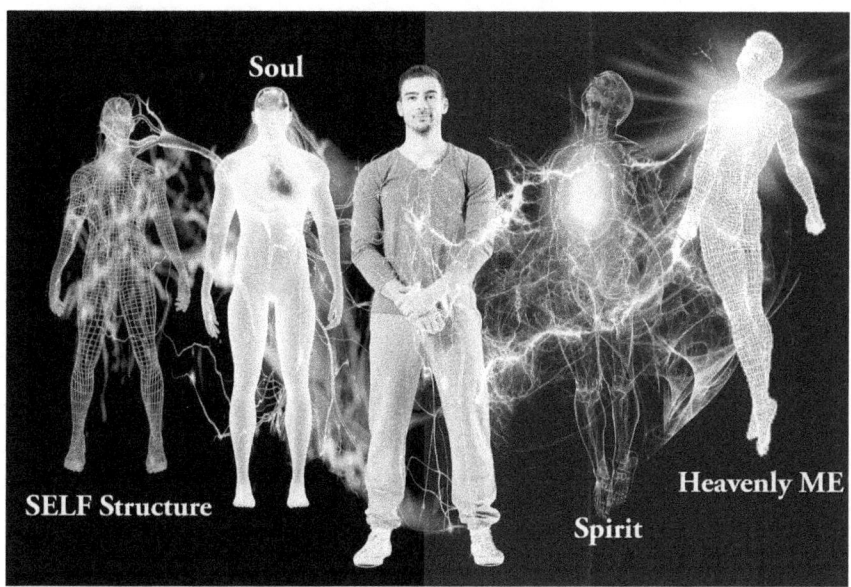

The Two Personas

> Therefore, put to death your members which are on the earth: fornication, uncleanness, passion, evil desire, and covetousness, which is idolatry. Because of these things the wrath of God is coming upon the sons of disobedience, in which you yourselves once walked when you lived in them.
>
> But now you yourselves are to put off all these: anger, wrath, malice, blasphemy, filthy language out of your mouth.
>
> Do not lie to one another, since you have put off the old mand with his deeds, and have put **on the**

> **new man** who is renewed in knowledge according to the image of Him who created him,
>
> | Colossians 3:5-10

4 | The Luminous Body

Let's review how Jesus describes that inner light a little more:

> "No one, when he has lit a lamp, puts it in a secret place or under a basket, but on a lampstand, that those who come in may see the light.
>
> The lamp of the body is the eye. Therefore, when your eye is good, your whole body also is full of light. But when your eye is bad, your body also is full of darkness.
>
> Therefore, take heed that the light which is in you is not darkness. If then **your whole body** is full of light, having no part dark, **the whole body will be full of light,** as when the bright shining of a lamp gives you light."
>
> | Luke 11:33-36

For my eyes to be good and full of light, I need to set my focus on Heaven and the dimensions of light.

As we have already stated, wherever I set my focus, my consciousness and level of light will also be.

My eyes will be good whenever I see things through God's redemptive eyes. Wherever there is sickness, I see wholeness. Wherever there is poverty, I see hope and divine provision. Wherever there is trouble, I see peace coming down from Heaven.

But if I set my focus on affliction, hopelessness, fear, and all I see is evil conspiring against me; if my heart is filled with lovelessness seeing the wicked going to hell; if all that is prophesied is destruction on the earth and our mouth utters fear and control over people, it will undoubtedly be a heart filled with darkness and not God. And since darkness is seen through those eyes, the body will be filled with it also.

Many may say: I have the light, but their mouth and deeds speak fear and anxiety.

If then your whole body is full of light, **having no part dark***, the entire body will be full of light,* (Luke 11:36)

We need to discern where our thoughts are coming from, and where is our focus?

The Father of lights is calling all the luminaries to unite, both in the Heavens and on the Earth.

5 | What Is From Above Overcomes the World

The hardest part of understanding Jesus is that He is not of this world nor is His Kingdom. He is rooted in Heaven and on the principles from above. We come from the Earth and have been formed by the principles of this world.

Jesus and the system in which we live have two completely different languages and two opposing foundations.

On one occasion, Jesus told the Pharisees:

> And He said to them, "You are from beneath; **I am from above**. You are of this world; **I am not of this world.**
>
> | John 8:23

Again, He expresses this same principle when He prays to the Father for those who believe in Him to be one with them.

> Now **I am no longer in the world**, but these are in the world, and I come to You. Holy Father, keep through Your name, those whom You have given Me, that they may be one as We are.
>
> | John 17:11

When Jesus Christ rose from the dead, He did not remain on the Earth, for the resurrection carries in itself an ascension into the heavens. It's a power that pulls you upwards. It's the power that caught Paul into the third heaven, and John, when Christ in His glory told him, "Come Up," and he entered through the eternal gates into the dimension of God's Throne Room.

When Christ enfolds you and absorbs you into Him, into the Resurrection Light, you ascend to reconnect to your heavenly being in the high places. This way you can also be from above and not below.

What is above has the power to raise what is below. Jesus imparts His life and resurrection into us, and it is

His life in us that He takes up to where He is. He takes us back to Him through our resurrected spirits.

> In My Father's house are many mansions; if it were not so, I would have told you. I go to prepare a place for you. And if I go and prepare a place for you,
>
> I will come again **and receive you to Myself**; that where I am, there you may be also.
>
> | **John 14:2-3**

What is from above overcomes the world, the system of lies. Truth is from above; lies and chaos are from below. The Spirit is from above and leads us into all Truth. The Truth sanctifies us because it transforms us into that which is from above. We are washed by the Word, by the Living Word, and plucked from falsehood and chaos.

Truth, love, the illumination of all that is spiritual and freedom, all dwell above. Life,is knowing the Father through Jesus Christ. It is where we find rest to see and hear the Father.

What is from above rises because it has no weight. The wind and the breath of God are from above. So those born of God have no weight in themselves because they carry within the weight of glory that is not subject to gravity.

The Truth hurls us into itself to no longer be of this world. It sanctifies us, immersing us in what is holy and separated from the mind of this world. The system can be conquered, bent, and defeated, but the Truth, never.

> Jesus says: "Whoever has come to know the world has found a corpse. And whoever has found (this) corpse, of him the world is not worthy."
>
> | **Thomas 56 (Apocrypha)**

True saints humble the system in their humility. They conquer lies with the truth, materialism with detachment and generosity, and the foolish rivalry of an egocentric system with divine love that does not seek its own but only to please the Father continually.

Truth is the substance; it is true. If you abide in my word, the truth shall set you free. It frees us from this system, from this system's bondage because of the fear of death that sustains it.

The true fills what is not so; substance fills the void. Truth is the light that dispels darkness. Love is light and is the substance of truth.

When we return to our original state, immersed in Christ Jesus, in sublime marriage and union to Him, we can call those who are below to once again enter into the dimensions of heaven, which are the Kingdom of God.

Chapter 8

THE RAQIA'S GOVERNMENT

1 | The Supreme Court of the Heavenly City

Let us now see the union between luminaries and the living creatures in the Raqia, and how they operate in the heavens and the Earth, to rule and govern together with the Sons of God.

To whom did God give the government and dominion of all things? In the beginning, He gave it to Adam, but he lost the kingdom. Once the second Adam, who is Christ, was crowned, He received it once again and gave it to His saints.

The government's operation in the Raqia's is clearly seen when John, while in the Spirit, sees an open door in Heaven and ascends to the heavenly dimensions of God's Throne.

Within the city of the Living God is the throne of God, and around it, the Supreme Court of Justice in Heaven. Here, we see Christ as the Lamb and the Lion of Judah, the living beings, and the twenty-four elders. They are the ones who will be able to read and execute God's judgments to bring justice to the Earth..

> Around the throne were twenty-four thrones, and on the thrones, I saw twenty-four elders sitting, clothed in white robes and they had crowns of gold on their heads.
>
> Before the throne there was a sea of glass, like crystal. And in the midst of the throne, and around the throne, were four living creatures full of eyes in front and in back.
>
> | **Revelation 4:4 & 6**

This is the governmental role of the New Jerusalem. Wherever the throne is, there will also be government, justice, and His Judgements' execution. For a city to be considered such, it must have a government with all its branches, agencies, and administration of its treasures.

The twenty-four elders represent those who have received the power to rule, govern, and judge as luminaries.

The number twenty-four is symbolic, representing all those established in the New Jerusalem, who received their heavenly garments, and now rule over the day and the night, separating light from the darkness. These are not just twenty-four, but hundreds or thousands from every nation.

> And they sang a new song, saying: *"You are worthy to take the scroll, and to open its seals; For You were slain, and have redeemed us to God by Your blood,* ***out of every tribe and tongue and people and nation. And have made us kings and priests to our God; and we shall reign on the earth."***
>
> | **Revelation 5:9-10**

> But the court shall be seated.... then the kingdom and dominion, and the greatness of the kingdoms under the whole heaven, shall be given to the people, the saints of the Most High. His kingdom is an everlasting kingdom, and all dominions shall serve and obey Him.'
>
> | **Daniel 7:26a, 27**

They are the ruling Raqia, the luminaries, whose Light, justice, and mercy shone on the earth and were found worthy to sit on the thrones.

> And I saw thrones, and they sat on them, and judgment was committed to them.
>
> | **Revelation 20:4a**

John can interact with them because he also is a ruling luminary.

Luminaries collect the saints' prayers and produce the symphony of all the stars when they worship God.

Early in the morning, when the dawn begins to awaken, and the soul becomes still and enters into God's divine rest, one can hear the song of the stars. When they worship, all creation listens. Gradually, they begin to awaken the birds' sounds and the harmony of every creature in the woods, mountains, and valleys, until all, in one accord, raise their lofty worship to the Creator.

Enoch saw the luminaries' mansions and the treasures given to them.

> And they took and brought me to a place in which **those who were there were like flaming fire, and, when they wished, they appeared as men**.
>
> And they brought me to the place of darkness, and to a mountain the point of whose summit reached to heaven. And I saw **the places of the luminaries and the treasuries of the stars** and of the thunder and in the uttermost depths, where were 4 a fiery bow and arrows and their quiver, and a fiery sword and all the lightnings.
>
> And they took me to the living waters, and to the fire of the west, which receives every setting of the sun.
>
> | **Enoch 17:1-4**

The luminaries' mansions are by the sides of Sheol because their mission is to separate the light from the darkness. These mansions form a wall of light to keep the darkness from advancing on the earth at will.

2 | The Raqia Executes God's Judgements

When the luminaries gather in heaven to execute justice, they meet in the heavens to determine which strata of the Raqia is to be shaken. When stars lose their dignity and radiance, they are dismissed. Then the Raqia, in the heavens, is rolled up like a scroll.

Every man, good or bad, has a star, but all are not established in God's Raquia. As the Prophet Daniel prophesied:

> Those who are wise shall shine, like the brightness of the firmament (Raqia), and those who turn many to righteousness kike the stars forever and ever.
>
> | Daniel 12:3

When the Son of Righteousness shines, and the light of His Raqia illuminates the earth, His mercy stretches forth, falling anew, every morning, on the just and unjust. But when God acts on the wicked, the sun and moon darken to give place to His wrath and justice.

> The sun shall be turned into darkness, and the moon into blood, before the coming of the great and awesome day of the Lord.
>
> | **Joel 2:31**

These judgments apply both to angelic beings and the prominent and wicked of the earth.

> I looked when He opened the sixth seal, and behold, there was a great earthquake; and the sun became black as sackcloth of hair, and the moon became like blood. And the stars of heaven fell to the earth, as a fig tree drops its late figs when it is shaken by a mighty wind.
>
> Then the sky receded as a scroll when it is rolled up, and every mountain and island was moved out of its place. And the kings of the earth, the great men, the rich men, the commanders, the mighty men, every slave and every free man, hid themselves in the caves and in the rocks of the mountains,
>
> | **Revelation 6:12-15**

This judgment we read about here was carried out with Jerusalem's destruction in the year 70AD. At that moment, the wrath of God came upon all those who had opposed and crucified Christ. The stars of Israel's mighty men and those of their oppressors –the Roman Empire– fell like figs from a fig tree when it is shaken.

When the heavens rolled up, and the stars fell, great chaos engulfed the earth. Kings, the mighty men, and all who followed in conflict fled to the caves, seeking to hide from God's wrath.

This is also the crowning moment when satan is thrown out of heaven, along with his angels that made up one-third of the stars –all finally cast down to earth.

> "And there will be signs in the sun, in the moon, and in the stars; and on the earth distress of nations, with perplexity, the sea and the waves roaring; men's hearts failing them from fear and the expectation of those things which are coming on the earth, for the powers of the heavens will be shaken.
>
> **| Luke 21:25-26**

Satan's name was Lucifer, son of the morning. He was the cherub responsible for carrying God's light and had access to God's throne in the Shamayim and the Raqia, along with all the angelic armies of the firmament.

> "How you are fallen from heaven (Shamayim), O Lucifer, son of the morning! How you are cut down to the ground, you who weakened the nations! For you have said in your heart:
>
> 'I will ascend into heaven (Shamayim). I will exalt my throne above (the Raquia) **the stars of God**. I will also sit on the mount of the congregation, on the farthest sides of the north.
>
> **| Isaiah 14:12-13**

We see several interesting things here. First, that satan wants to place his throne above God's Raqia, and the other that he used his heavenly position to weaken the nations.

By this, we understand that angels, in their positions as stars and luminaries, can directly impact the earth's events.

In this passage, we also see that he refers to the angels as "sons of God" and "stars of God." If there were only stars of God, there would be no need to call them this way, and just stars would do. Therefore, there are stars of God and others that are not His.

Enoch describes how the stars became defiled. Additionally, they attach to men's thoughts when they are worshiped.

> And many chiefs of the stars shall transgress the order (prescribed). And these shall alter their orbits and tasks, and not appear at the seasons prescribed to them.
>
> And the whole order of the stars shall be concealed from the sinners, and the thoughts of those on the earth shall err concerning them, [and they shall be altered from all their ways, yea, they shall err and take them to be gods.
>
> And evil shall be multiplied upon them, and punishment shall come upon them So as to destroy all.'
>
> | **Enoch 80:6-8**

> And all the luminaries shall be affrighted with great fear,
>
> And all the earth shall be affrighted and tremble and be alarmed. And all the angels shall execute their command and shall seek to hide themselves from the presence of the Great Glory, and the children of earth shall tremble and quake.
>
> | **Enoch 102:2-3**

For someone to exercise government and dominion, they need to be established in the Raqia.

Satan lost this place eternally and forever, as did his angels. They are no more than abominable plunder and refuse, stripped of all government and authority, continually defeated by the wise (those with understanding) of the Lord.

God is bringing His judgment on both angels and men.

And another sign appeared in heaven: behold, a great, fiery red dragon having seven heads and ten horns, and seven diadems on his heads. His tail drew a **third of the stars of heaven and threw them to the earth.**

> And war broke out in heaven: Michael and his angels fought with the dragon; and the dragon and his angels fought, but they did not prevail, nor was a place found for them in heaven any longer.
>
> So the great dragon was cast out, that serpent of old, called the Devil and Satan, who deceives

> the whole world; he was cast to the earth, and his angels were cast out with him.
>
> Then I heard a loud voice saying in heaven, "Now salvation, and strength, and the kingdom of our God, and the power of His Christ have come, for the accuser of our brethren, who accused them before our God day and night, has been cast down.
>
> And they overcame him by the blood of the Lamb and by the word of their testimony, and they did not love their lives to the death.

| **Revelation 12:3-4ª & 7-11**

In this great battle waged in the heavens, we see not only Michael and his angels engaging in battle but also the interaction of the saints in Heavenly places that were instrumental in satan's fall and Michael's victory....they have overcome!

These events taking place in the heavens is part of the scene we looked at earlier, with John, the 24 elders, and the four living creatures before God's Throne.

The Lamb opened the seals to issue sentences and have His judgments executed. This is how God's Raqia operates in conjunction with God's stars (heavenly hosts), the living creatures, and the luminaries.[54].

As God executes His judgments, the living creatures and the governing sons of God –represented by the 24 elders and the thousands upon thousands of angels– all worship.

[54] - Revelation 5:5-10

This worship that proceeds from the heavenly places emits the necessary light to awaken every living being to recognize their position in God and worship Him.

> Saying with a loud voice: "Worthy is the Lamb who was slain to receive power and riches and wisdom, and strength and honor and glory and blessing!"
>
> **And every creature which is in heaven and on the earth and under the earth and such as are in the sea, and all that are in them, I heard saying:** "Blessing and honor and glory and power be to Him who sits on the throne, and to the Lamb, forever and ever!"
>
> | **Revelation 5:12-13**

That is why King David, who was the light of Israel[55], the luminary who shone the Father's Light, wrote:

> Praise the Lord **from the heavens**;
> **Praise Him in the heights**!
>
> Praise Him, all His angels;
> Praise Him, all His hosts!
>
> Praise Him, sun and moon;
> Praise Him, **all you stars of light!**
>
> | **Psalms 148:1-3**

---

[55] - 2 Samuel 21:17

The worship of those in the New Jerusalem takes place in the heavens. These are those the wise who shine with the brightness of Christ's Light. They are called the bright stars.

Some stars go out, or they are cast out, but others shine and beam. We are not talking about a star's natural light in the firmament, but the Light that came into this world. Indeed, the life of men from which all understanding of the heavenly proceeds. The Light of the first Day that gave men the rule and dominion over all creation.

God wants to establish His true Raqia through His Sons of Light. He wants to cause the Son of Righteousness to shine and rule over the earth, illuminating every man through the Sons of Light.

Chapter 9

REST: THE KEY TO ACCESS HEAVENLY DIMENSIONS

Because the perfection of the totality is in the Father, it is requisite that they all ascend unto him. When someone recognizes, he receives the things that are his own and gathers them to himself.

For he who is unacquainted has a lack—and what he lacks is great, since what he lacks is Him who will make him perfect. Because the perfection of the totality is in the Father, it is requisite that

> they all ascend unto him. Thus each and every one receives himself.
>
> **| Valentinus 11 (Apocrypha)**

This totality is (the Pleroma,) the fulness of which John speaks:

> And of His fullness we have all received, and grace for grace. For the law was given through Moses, but grace and truth came through Jesus Christ.
>
> No one has seen God at any time. The only begotten Son, who is in the bosom of the Father, He has declared Him.
>
> **| John 1:16-18**

One finds the knowledge of the Father in rest. In this state of the soul and spirit, the Father makes everything visible and accessible in His Kingdom. In this stillness, He imparts His Nature, and we see Him face to face and turn to Him.

> Yeshua says, "If you do not abstain from the world[56], you will not find the kingdom. If you do not make the entire week into a Sabbath, you will not behold the Father."
>
> **| Thomas 27 (Apocrypha)**[57]

---

[56] Unless you refrain from being nourished by the system.

[57] www.metalog.org/print/Metagosp.pdf

The Raqia Reflected on The Earth

I made this illustration for you to see the impact of a soul at rest.

Notice how the Raqia is reflected on Earth when the waters, (representing the soul) are in complete stillness. This is why it is so important to enter into God's rest. It is transcendent for the Lord since He created our heavenly being to reflect His nature on the Earth.

When our waters are choppy or turbulent, they cannot reflect heaven. That is why it is vital to understand that the voice that comes from the Light brings joy, peace, and rest.

The Kingdom of God will never speak anything to terrify us. Whenever God uttered a prophetic word of correction to Israel in the Old Testament, along with it, He gave them a solution.

But today, the waters of the world are extremely turbulent because many prophecies are filled with fear and anxiety. God needs beings of Light willing to reflect the supernatural peace of Christ in this world.

This is truly powerful if you can understand and embrace what I'm trying to communicate to you. By simply entering into God's rest, we become gateways for everything heavenly to manifest on the Earth.

We are the doors for the heavenly to manifest on the earth.

It is in the Raqia that we find all the armies of God Almighty. When we quieten our soul and enter a state of peace and stillness, our waters reflect what takes place in the Raqia. We set in motion all the actions and designs that God is releasing on the earth. And even any possible judgments that God might bring upon the world, we view them from a position of peace and not turmoil.

Activism doesn't release heaven on the earth, but it is a state of complete stillness, in our soul and spirit, that causes God to manifest Himself.

Previously, we saw how satan, after man's fall, created a false Raqia, a lying illusion akin to the heavenly reality, and placed his fallen angels therein.

He seeks to instigate men to worship these demons in the form of the sun, moon, and stars to emulate the way heaven acts on earth. And to achieve this, satan creates a magical mirage granting men access through meditation and demonic trances.

The forces of darkness train their own priests, people sensitive to the spiritual realm, to enter the dimensions of this false Raqia and release their power on them.

They know perfectly well that the soul is used for earthly passions but that it can also emulate the human spirit. This is why we see wizards and sorcerers, people from spiritualistic and oriental cultures, practice transcendental meditation. This practice consists of entering into a metaphysical silence that connects them with what they call the universe. However, this is nothing else than the false Raqia created to imitate the power of God and His rest.

The new age and magical sciences continually activate this false Raqia, thereby bringing the power of darkness upon the earth.

Although the devil and his kingdom have been defeated forevermore, his works continue affecting all who remain under this world's system.

God needs us to truly become the sons of the Day, with an understanding of how to operate in the dimensions of Light and undo all the devil's works.

So when Jesus speaks to us, saying, you are the Light of the world, He sees us through God's eyes before the foundation of the world, where we were the lights that had emerged from the Father, as the sons of God in Light.

1 | Rest And Joy

> The light of the eyes rejoices the heart.
>
> | **Proverbs 15:30a**

We saw earlier that the word for light in this proverb is the same as luminary, *"Maor."* So, in the illustration at the beginning of this chapter, our heavenly luminary is directly connected to our Spirit. That light that emanates from us carries joy within itself that fills the heart. It is the Light of God's Kingdom, righteousness, peace, and joy in the Spirit. So when I reflect that light on the earth, I bring the Kingdom of God to wherever I am.

Think of how much the earth is in need, right now, of beings of light that project peace and joy? The joy and happiness that come from Heaven are nothing short of a magnificent light.

It's like a couple's glow on their wedding day. They radiate with hearts filled with so much love and joy that everything in them becomes light.

True joy and true happiness result from being in that place of rest in God, where we receive all His blessings and see every glorious thing that God has prepared for us.

> The light of the righteous rejoices, but the lamp of the wicked will be put out.
>
> | **Proverbs 13:9**

Light has the ability to rejoice in itself and fill our hearts with joy, but it has to do with those free of all bitterness and rancor. These are those that have conquered sorrow unto death and the sin that leads to darkness. They are the ones that have crucified their lusts and their flesh and have denied themselves the right to be offended and enraged.

2 | The Path To Joy

One morning I Heard the Voice of God in the waters of the sea. Words emerged out of the motion of the waves like a language that became clear to my understanding. And they said:

Gentle and merciful are the ways of those who seek me, and I fill them with my joy. Just then, the sea hit hard and added: *but I need to send my waves to break the rocks in the hearts of those who resist Me.*

He then went on to speak to me about the water and the light. *I use water to shatter the rocks of the soul. Water erodes and breaks every stone, but the light is meant for transparent hearts. When light runs into a rock, it cannot pass through and prevents it from reaching the spirit. Light only penetrates the transparent souls. The pure of heart are those who see me.*

3 | True Joy

One of the most inspiring characters of history, for me, is Francis of Assisi. Hopefully, one day, God will allow me to write about his original texts, stripped of the corruption in which they were later engulfed. The extraordinary fellowship he enjoyed with Christ helped restore the knowledge of Jesus to Europe, which had been utterly lost in the 13th. Century.

He lived in a time when all there was in Western Europe was the Catholic Church. There were no Bibles, no teachers, and no pastors to help. It was just he and God against one of the darkest generations ever to live on the Earth. He nourished himself with a copy of the gospels, translated into Italian, which came to his hands by a fellow prisoner during the war in Assisi.

John, that was his real name also known with the nickname of Francesco, inspired by the rich young ruler's passage, decided to renounce all material possessions in this world to follow the gospel to the letter. He suffered in unspeakable ways, and as is common in a perverse society, was often persecuted, slandered, and beaten by the wicked.

One of the most amazing things about his life was that he still was one of the happiest men of his time despite not having anything in this world. The joy of the Lord was with Him always, continually supplying for all his needs. He understood that he already had everything.

I want to share an extract with you of his view of happiness:

"How St Francis, walking one Day with Brother Leo, Explained to Him what Things Perfect Joy are:

> One day in winter, as St Francis was going with Brother Leo from Perugia to St Mary of the Angels, and was suffering greatly from the cold, he called to Brother Leo, who was walking on before him, and said to him:
>
> If, when we shall arrive at St Mary of the Angels, all drenched with rain and trembling with cold, all covered with mud and exhausted from hunger; if, when we knock at the convent-gate, the porter should come angrily and ask us who we are; if, after we have told him, we are two of the brethren', he should answer angrily, What you say is not the truth; you are but two impostors going about to deceive the world, and take away the alms of the poor; begone I say'; if then he refuse to open to us, and leave us outside, exposed to the snow and rain, suffering from cold and hunger till nightfall - then, if we accept such injustice, such cruelty and such contempt with patience, without being ruffled and without murmuring, believing with humility and charity that the porter really knows us, and that it is God who made him to speak thus against us, write down, O Brother Leo, that this is perfect joy.

And if we knock again, and the porter come out in anger to drive us away with oaths and blows, as if we were vile impostors, saying, Begone, miserable robbers! to the hospital, for here you shall neither eat nor sleep!' - and if we accept all this with patience, with joy, and with charity, O Brother Leo, write that this indeed is perfect joy.

And if, urged by cold and hunger, we knock again, calling to the porter and entreating him with many tears to open to us and give us shelter, for the love of God, and if he come out more angry than before, exclaiming, These are but importunate rascals, I will deal with them as they deserve'; and taking a knotted stick, he seize us by the hood, throwing us on the ground, rolling us in the snow, and shall beat and wound us with the knots in the stick - if we bear all these injuries with patience and joy, thinking of the sufferings of our Blessed Lord, which we would share out of love for him, write, O Brother Leo, that here, finally, is perfect joy.

And now, brother, listen to the conclusion. Above all the graces and all the gifts of the Holy Spirit which Christ grants to his friends, is the grace of overcoming oneself, and accepting willingly, out of love for Christ, all suffering, injury, discomfort and contempt; for in all other gifts of God we cannot glory, seeing they proceed not from ourselves but from God, according to the words of the Apostle, what have you, that you have not received from God? and if you have received it, why do you glory for as if you had not received it? But in the cross of tribulation and affliction we may glory, because, as the Apostle says again, I will not glory save in the cross of our Lord Jesus Christ."

Reading this level of the cross rattles every thought of the modern Gospel riddled with concessions, comforts, self-pity, and fears of people anxious for the things of this world.

Valentinus pens something beautiful concerning this that several of us have had the joy of experiencing, so real that any moral or physical pain simply fades away.

> And happy is the man who comes to himself and awakens. Indeed, blessed is he who has opened the eyes of the blind. And the Spirit (Ruaj)[58] came to him in haste when he raised him. Having given its hand to the one lying prone on the ground, it placed him firmly on his feet,[59] for he had not yet stood up. He gave them the means of knowing the knowledge of the Father and the revelation of his son. For when they saw it and listened to it, he permitted them to take a taste of and to smell and to grasp the beloved son
>
> | **Valentinus 28 (Aprocrypha)**

4 | Joy Changes Every Circumstance

Rome Experience

On one occasion, we were headed to a spiritual mission in Iraq.

---

[58] - Ruaj hakodesh, is the word for Holy Spirit in the Hebrew.

[59] - The word hakodesh is the feminine term for Kadosh. Then the Hebrew expresses the Holy Spirit in the feminine tense.

Our mission was to deliver the nation from Sadam Hussein's oppression and open the country's doors to the Gospel.

We finally succeeded, as history shows, and the Gospel made it in through the American troops.

The team consisted of just five women, and we were in Rome ready to fly a plane to Jordan, as the airport in Baghdad was closed due to the embargo.[60]

One of our intercessors, Oriana, was Columbian, and when we arrived at the counter to check our tickets, the agent said in a rude and impolite way that she could not travel, arguing that her name wasn't in the system.

I immediately countered by stating that we were a group, and all five tickets had been purchased together. The agent got even angrier, further insisting that she wasn't in the system.

My spiritual eyes were opened at that moment, and I saw a large number of demons all around the agent's computer. Then I heard the voice of the Holy Spirit clearly tell me: Rejoice, sing, and dance!

And without a second thought about how ridiculous it might seem, we started to sing and dance and laugh at the airport. Gradually the demonic activity came to a halt. The Light of rejoicing started manifesting in us. Angels were immediately activated, while the agents of darkness were left crippled.

His glorious Light emanated from us, invisible to the natural eye but very visible in the spirit. Suddenly, the

---

[60] - Iraq came under embargo when it lost Persian Gulf War against the United States in 1990

man cried out, "Oh, her name, Oriana, is right here in our system!"

It was one of the most wonderful lessons we could have received before entering Iraq. Because five women entering that country, alone, during Sadam Hussein's time, could have been a source of great distress. But God taught us a valuable lesson to triumph in that war with the Light of His Joy!

Chapter 10

WHAT MANIFESTS ON THE EARTH DEPENDS ON US

Our eyes are the lamp of our soul. Our way of seeing, thinking, and understanding God will determine the level of light that comes out of us.

When we truly set our sight on God, we will see everything redemptively. When God looks at our fallen world, He sees it covered in the blood of His Son, which day and night speaks of the mercy that overcomes judgment.

> So, speak and so do as those who will be judged by the law of liberty.

> For judgment is without mercy to the one who has shown no mercy. Mercy triumphs over judgment.
>
> | **James 2:12-13**

As we imagine God's heart, with over five billion unsaved people, at this moment of history, could He possibly be looking to destroy the world and send it to hell?

This thought, which underpins the vast majority of fatalistic prophecies heard today, is dark indeed. That is why we need to understand what the true Light and love of God really are.

The Light of the righteous shall rejoice. And as I write this, my spirit can see waves of Light flowing out of the heart of God upon the people. There is an anointing of joy and gladness coming upon all those who open their hearts to live by His Light. It will be their fortress in the times to come, which are not for destruction but to straighten the path of many.

Death is only for those who choose to live by death. But some of the righteous will even be taken to heaven, because God needs them to operate from there.

God is calling us to His Light, enter therein. God needs you as a son of Light, right now, to transform the earth and be a hope and a provision for the times of tribulations that are to come.

If you wish to be a servant of God during these times, choose to be a servant of the Light and peace that surpasses all understanding. Produce righteousness, joy, and uprightness in people.

> For nothing is secret that will not be known, nor anything hidden that will not be known and come to light.
>
> | **Luke 8:17**

After reading this passage, some might believe that God is talking about exposing our faults or our sins. But thinking this way only reveals how our natural eyes view this scripture.

Jesus is talking about the light that lies hidden within us. It is what we are according to our heavenly being since before the foundation of the world; that wonderful being, full of light, with your star beaming above you, manifesting the Kingdom of God on the Earth. Perhaps you have never seen yourself like this, but it will surely manifest this way because Jesus Christ prophesied it.

Like the illustration in the previous chapter, you will also manifest likewise, and the world will start to see you this way.

> Therefore, thus says the Lord: "If you return, then I will bring you back. You shall stand before Me. **If you take out the precious from the vile, you shall be as My mouth**.
>
> Let them return to you, but you must not return to them. And I will make you to this people a fortified bronze wall. And they will fight against you, but they shall not prevail against you; for I am with you to save you and deliver you," says the Lord.

> "I will deliver you from the hand of the wicked, and I will redeem you from the grip of the terrible."
>
> **| Jeremiah 15:19-21**

Because everything hidden within you, that glorious life that is Christ in you, will be manifested.

Now, what do we need to do to make it manifest in our life?

For something to manifest on the earth, someone has to believe it!

So if I enter into God's rest, if I still my soul and start to believe that all that I am, everything in my eternal self, is going to manifest, that is precisely what will happen.

Jesus went on to say something very significant after announcing how the light would manifest all things..

> Therefore, take heed how you hear. For whoever has to him more will be given; and whoever does not have, even what he seems to have will be taken from him."
>
> **| Luke 8:18**

TAKE HEED HOW YOU HEAR! If God is urging you to enter into His rest, to know Him in His Light, to connect to your spiritual being, take heed then how you hear!

Contemplate Heaven, all you sons of Heaven, and all the works of the Most High.[61]

---

[61] - Enoch 101:1

Now I don't have a direct transcription of the Hebrew for this passage from Enoch, but when it talks about Heaven and all the works of the Most High, he is very likely referring to the Raqia since that is where He created all the hosts of Heaven.

So, I could translate it this way: Think carefully on God's Throne and the Raqia, and in all the works of the Most High that proceed from it.

Jesus' focus was on Heaven, which is why His Light provided salvation for the entire world.

His mind was never caught up in the torrent of persecution, and wickedness uttered against him. And indeed, he was often discouraged at the sight of the people in such darkness, even telling them, *"O faithless and perverse generation, how long shall I be with you? How long shall I bear with you?*[62] But He never stayed stuck on that thought. He immediately rose to the place from where He was from, from above.

And this is the place the Father is calling the sons of the Kingdom to be established, so they, in turn, can reach out to a lost generation.

The Light of Christ shines to manifest everything. My prayer is that once it manifests on you, all it finds is its own light.

THE END

[62] - Matthew 17:17

APPENDIX 1

HISTORY OF THE CANONS

The word canon is a term that implies a straight rod or a reed. There are many applications where it is used as an "instrument of measurement," and Biblically, it is used to determine the books that make up the Holy Scriptures.

In fact, there are several canons. Our Bibles use the one that was established by the Catholic Church in the IV Century. Later, Martin Luther eliminated the Apocrypha from them, also known as the Deuterocanonical books.

The New Testament canons of the Western Catholic, Protestant, Orthodox, Coptic, Armenian, Ethiopian, and

Syrian/Nestorian differ significantly from each other–and the various branches of Christianity didn't discuss these lists until many centuries after Christ.

During the first centuries, the idea of combining the books and the apostolic letters revolved around diverse opinions of prominent leaders located in different geographical areas. The church multiplied organically without having a form or organization to submit to. Communication wasn't as it is today, and as the Gospel continued to spread throughout Europe, Africa, and Asia, the churches adopted different forms. Not all were dependent on Rome. The Coptic church in Egypt and the Ethiopian and Sirian churches were independent and very relevant.

As a result, opinions concerning the texts widely accepted today are quite varied. Other manuscripts were circulating at that time, such as the Shepherd of Hermas, Gospel of the Egyptians, Gospel of Thecla, Gospel of Peter, the Traditions of Matthias, the Revelation of Peter, the Didascalia and the Acts of Paul and others.

Thus, from the middle of the fourth century, the Sinaiticus Codex includes Barnabas[63] and the Shepherd of Hermas.[64] At the same time, the Alexandrine Codex, from the turn of the V Century, contains I & II Clement and the Psalms of Solomon.

In his book, "Lost Scriptures," Dr. Bart Ehrman[65] whom due to his research in early Christianity, received the Magna Cum Laude Award from Princeton Theological Seminary, wrote:

---

[63] - This is certainly a heretical epistle and we do not approve it.

[64] - This is a text that shows catholic principles which are not in accordance to the Bible nor with Evangelical Christian thought.

[65] - Dr Bart Ehrman graduated from Wheaton College in Illinois. It was at Princeton Theological Seminary that he received his doctorate.

"The Gospels that came to be included in the New Testament were all written anonymously; only at a later time were they called by the names of their re puted authors, Matthew, Mark, Luke, and John. But at about the time these names were being associated with the Gospels, other Gospel books were be coming available, sacred texts that were read and revered by different Chris tian groups throughout the world: a Gospel, for example, claiming to be written by Jesus' closest disciple, Simon Peter; another by his apostle Philip; a Gospel allegedly written by Jesus' female disciple Mary Magdalene; another by his own brother, Didymus Judas Thomas.

Someone decided that four of these early Gospels, and no others, should be accepted as part of the canon—the collection of sacred books of Scripture. But how did they make their decisions? When? How can we be sure they were right? And whatever happened to the other books?

When the New Testament was finally gathered together, it included Acts, an account of the activities of the disciples after Jesus' death. But there were other Acts written in the early years of the church: the Acts of Peter and of John, the Acts of Paul, the Acts of Paul's female companion Thecla, and others. Why were these not included as parts of Scripture?

Our New Testament today contains a number of epistles, that is, letters writ ten by Christian leaders to other Christians, thirteen of them allegedly by Paul. Scholars debate whether Paul actually wrote all of these letters. And there are other letters not in the New Testament that also claim to be written by Paul, for example, several letters sent by "Paul" to the Roman philosopher Seneca, and a letter written to the church of Laodicea, and Paul's Third Corinthians (the New Testament has First and Second Corinthians). Moreover, there were letters written in the names of other apostles as well, including one allegedly written by Simon Peter to Jesus' brother James, and another by Paul's companion Barnabas. Why were these excluded?

But why were other apocalypses not admitted into the canon, such as the apocalypse allegedly written by Simon Peter, in which he is given a guided tour of heaven and hell to see the glorious ecstasies of the saints and, described in yet more graphic detail, the horrendous torments of the damned? Or the book popular among Christian readers of the second century, the Shepherd of Hermas, which, like the book of Revelation, is filled with apocalyptic visions of a prophet?

We now know that at one time or another, in one place or another, all of these noncanonical books and many others were revered as sacred, inspired, scriptural. Some of them we now have; others we know only by name. Only twenty-seven of the early Christian books were finally included in the canon, copied by scribes through the ages, eventually translated into English, and now on bookshelves in virtually every home in America. Other books came to be rejected, scorned, maligned, attacked, burned, all but forgotten—lost.[66]

---

[66] Lost Scriptures Dr. Bart Ehrman Pg 3-4

Some scholars believe that towards the end of the 2nd. Century, Irenaeus, bishop of Lyon, established the four gospels in churches affiliated to Rome, based on Muratori's codex list.

However, there was no council on the New Testament canon until the Laodicea Synod in 363 A.C., which ended up rejecting John's Book of Revelation.

Four years later, in 367 A.C., Athanasius, Bishop of Alexandria, presented a list of 27 books as those with authority to be part of the Canon. This letter, known as #39, didn't resolve the matter conclusively. However, ultimately, his point of view prevailed, and 26 books of his list were accepted, except for John's Revelation, which wasn't definitively confirmed until the Council of Trent in 1546 A.C..

Although episcopal councils, prudently, have never claimed to be infallible. The Trent vote was 24 to 15, with 16 abstentions. The various Protestant branches then accepted this list.

The many Eastern churches also have equally complicated histories establishing their respective New Testament Canons. For example, the Armenian Canon includes a 3rd. Pauline letter to the Corinthians. The Coptic New Testament contains I and II Clement. The Nestorian Peshitta excludes II and III John, Jude, and Revelation. And the Ethiopian Bible adds books called the Synods, the Epistle of Peter to Clement, the Book of the Covenant, and the Didascalia.

The events that transpired in the first three and a half centuries A.D., before the earliest ecclesiastical attempts to establish a canon, is markedly obscure since the

Messianics of the original gospel were finally supplanted by the "Christians" who debated in a continuous schism between the Pauline and Petrine traditions.

Justin Martir, considered one of the first Christian Apologists, completely ignored the Pauline Epistles.

At the end of the 2nd Century, Clement of Alexandria and Irenaeus of Lyon were the first authors to cite both the Gospels and Paul explicitly.

By this time, the Church Fathers had stopped being led by the Spirit and depended on their understanding. The Popes, whose theological decisions were deemed infallible, also emerged.

John reflects in his gospel and epistles a debate exposed to the early Christian about who Jesus is, insisting that Jesus is both man and divine –something not found in the other gospels. Together with his followers, Thomas also shares John's view, believing that the "divine light embodied by Jesus is shared by those who believe since we are all made" in the image of God."

Thomas's followers saw in him his apostolic authority, just as other Christians saw it in Peter, Paul, John, or James, the brother of Jesus.

The church was more Petrine than Pauline in its beginnings, and the Gospel of Peter was in higher circulation than Paul's letters, until its elimination in the end.

Dr. Ehrman continues his study by saying:

> "Prior to its discovery, virtually everything we knew about the Gospel of Peter came from Eusebius's

account. In his ten-volume Church History, Eusebius narrates the history of the Christian Church from the days of Jesus down to his own time, in the early fourth century. This writing is our best source for the history of Christianity after the period of the New Testament to the time of the emperor Constantine, the first Roman emperor to convert to Christianity. The work is filled with anecdotes and, of yet greater use to historians, extensive quotations of earlier Christian writings. In many instances, Eusebius's quota tions are our only source of knowledge of Christian texts from the second and third centuries[67]."

We need to understand that the Early Church did not have an immutable theological treatise to which all churches were subject.

Even in the 1st Century, before the destruction of Jerusalem in the year 70 AD, there was a document called the Didache or Didascalia[68], in circulation, a simple letter containing the basic apostolic instructions the church was to follow[69].

Many of the Didascalia's doctrinal points focus on the customs of that day in time and how Christians were to follow Christ's instructions in them.

There were also different types of churches expressing the manifold wisdom of God in different ways. This gave birth to various forms of true Christianity, always based on Christ's teachings and the Apostles' doctrine. Some of

---

[67] - Dr. Bart Ehrman, Lost christianities pg 14, Eusebius, Serapion, and the Gospel of Peter

[68] - http://solutionsagp.es/resources/Didache.pdf You can download it from this site.

[69] - (We can see some of the commandments directly related to Jewish customs concerning the lodging of travelers and the offerings to be offered due to faults committed. Faults are different from the forgiveness of sins which can only be washed by the blood of Christ.)

them had the Holy Spirit, others didn't, as in the book of Acts.

Bart D. Ehrman adds:

> "All this diversity of belief and practice, and the intolerance that occasionally results, makes it difficult to know whether we should think of Christianity as one thing or lots of things, whether we should speak of Christianity or Christianities.
>
> What could be more diverse than this variegated phenomenon, Christianity in the modern world? In fact, there may be an answer: Christianity in the ancient world. As historians have come to realize, during the first three Christian centuries, the practices and beliefs found among people who called themselves Christian were so varied that the differences between Roman Catholics, Primitive Baptists, and Seventh-Day Adventists pale by comparison.
>
> Most of these ancient forms of Christianity are unknown to people in the world today, since they eventually came to be reformed or stamped out. As a result, the sacred texts that some ancient Christians used to support their religious perspectives came to be proscribed, destroyed, or forgotten—in one way or another lost."

As Dr. Bart Ehrman states, there wasn't just one Christianity but many Christianities. The most prominent groups were the Ebionite Jewish Christians, the anti-Jewish Marists, some Gnostic Christians, and the Proto-orthodox Christians.

These types of divisions are also seen within Judaism. During Jesus' time, they were divided into three main groups: the Saducees, the Pharisees, and the Essenes. Bear in mind that there were no Bibles, nor were the Gospels written until the end of the first century. Furthermore, there was no printing press nor the internet to reproduce them. The vast majority of believers didn't have access to the Old Testament scrolls and even less so if they were Gentiles. This is why John encourages the church by writing:

> But you have an anointing from the Holy One, and you know all things.
> | **1 John 2:20**

John's followers were taught to depend entirely on the Holy Spirit. The most important things among them were to love God, love their neighbor, pray, remain in unity, and partake of the Lord's Supper.

But the other groups sought to hold on to the written Word, as was the case of the Galatians. Some were pro-Jewish and others anti-Jewish.

In the 2nd Century, Irenaeus, Bishop of Lyon in Roman Gaul[70], became the chief architect of what is known as the "Canon of the four Gospels," discarding many writings that could have been penned by the other apostles of Christ.

For Irenaeus, any spiritual experience that could lead towards the intuitive knowledge of our Heavenly Father was considered heretical. According to him, the Gospels must be rationally and practically discerned, not spiritually—this school of thought echoes to this day in

[70] - France

both the Catholic Church and many traditional Evangelical Churches.

The growing influence of heretical Gnosticism threatened the early church, which lacked a formal document such as the Bible and could easily go astray. In his struggle against Gnostic heretics, Irenaeus completely did away with the baptism in the Holy Spirit and a genuine experience with God. The church had to stay under a single immutable dogma that grouped the church under the Roman Bishopric as the sole and infallible authority to remain united.

We must understand that the majority of documents in circulation were written or translated into Greek. The knowledge of God Gnoseos tou Theou or the "Gnosis of God" was a central part of Christ's message. *And this is eternal life, that they may know You, the only true God, and Jesus Christ whom You have sent* (John 17:3)

Notice that by using the same Greek term, Gnosis, in the real knowledge of God, which is experiential and inherent in the Spirit, it was easy to get mixed up with the growing threat of Gnosticism, which proclaimed Gnosis or the knowledge of God without the need for a Savior. Man could save himself since he was made out of the same substance as God. Obviously, this was heresy. Gnosticism didn't recognize Jesus Christ as the sole mediator between God and man.

Therefore, under the stigma of "heretics," Irenaeus persecuted all those who professed to know God by the Spirit, placing them in the same Gnostics group. His great work was called "Against Heresies." And he burned every document he found that had to do with any spiritual experience to know God. This is why many texts were hidden and preserved, to avoid falling into the hands of Irenaeus.

As I mentioned earlier, in the IV Century, Athanasius, Bishop of Alexandria, who also shared Irenaeus' ideas, wrote a list of canonical books. His goal in creating it was to combat heresy and purge the church of the "Apocryphal" books that led believers astray. Unfortunately, he also did away with those that enlightened them.

Athanasius gave instructions on how to read canonical writings, imposing many dogmas that still remain in force in the Catholic Church today. Above all, he warned believers to avoid spiritual intuition. Athanasius declared it a deceptive ability that only leads to error, a position that the «Roman Church» endorsed then and maintained to this day[71].

In short, what we know today as the Bible Canon, was a list chosen by one man who never knew the Spirit of God and persecuted Him with all his might. In the first council of Laodicea, they simply accepted the book selection made by Athanasius.

Moreover, the Catholic Church forbid the reading of the old testament and of the new emerging testament.

Decree of the Council of Toulouse (1229 C.E.): "We prohibit also that the laity should be permitted to have the books of the Old or New Testament; but we most strictly forbid their having any translation of these books."[72]

---

[71] Athanasius' letter was translated into Coptic and read in all monasteries of Egypt. A great number of scholars agree that the Nag Hammadi codices found in 1945 had been buried by their owners as a result of Athanasius banning of heretical books. The owners in question were presumably monks from the Pachomian Monastery in ancient Chenoboskia.

[72] Bernard Starr, Contributor - College Professor (Emeritus, City University of N.Y), psychologist, journalist.

By no means am I saying that the Bible is false or unreliable, for it is the greatest treasure that we have. What a blessing that they did not discard the Gospel of John or Paul's incredibly spiritual letters.

What I am trying to say is that there are things that have been hidden, which God wants to bring to Light, that can be key to raise a true generation of Light.

APPENDIX 2

LOST BOOKS WORTH CONSIDERING

| The Book of Enoch

It appears between the Old and New Testament periods, three centuries before Christ. It's a part of the Bible Canon of the Coptic Church's Ethiopian and Eritrean patriarchies. Still, it is not recognized by the other Christian churches despite having been found in some of the Septuagint Codexes (Vatican Codex and Beatty Chester Papyrus). The Beta Isreal (Ethiopian Jews) include it in the Tanaj, contrary to other current Jews who exclude it.

Many early Christian groups considered the Book of Enoch to be a part of the Holy Scriptures. This is the reason why it is mentioned in the epistle to the Hebrews and the book of Jude. The writings of the so-called church fathers are full of references to this book. Justin Martyr, Irenaeus, Origins, and Clement of Alexandria all mention it as well. Tertullian (160-230) A.D. calls it "Holy Scripture," and the Ethiopian Church included it in its official canon. It was a well-known and widely read text during the first three centuries of our era, although later discredited at the Council of Laodicea 363-364 A.C.

After having remained forgotten for many centuries, it emerged once again with great interest during the Protestant Reformation.

The modern recovery of the Book of Enoch is due to explorer James Bruce, who, in 1773, after six years in Abyssinia, returned to England with the three Ethiopian copies of the book. The first English translation was published in 1821. Some Greek fragments of the text were later found at the turn of the XX Century. And finally, seven copies in Aramaic were discovered in the Dead Sea scrolls, although they were incomplete. The only complete manuscripts are in the Ethiopian language, with some portions found in Greek and Latin.

| The Melchizedek Scroll

Another book, parallel to the Bible's sacred writings, is the Melchizedek Scroll. It is one of the Dead Sea Scrolls, found in one of the Qumran caves, consisting of 7 scrolls sewn together.

According to scholars of the Dead Sea manuscripts, the first scroll in the compendium was written by Abraham, the patriarch of Israel. The book includes a wonderful depiction of Genesis, and the history of how the universe was formed before the world was.

| Gospel of Thomas

As for the date of composition of the original text, sometimes referred to as the "Fifth Gospel," no consensus exists among scholars. Some date the text as early as the first half of the First Century, even before the first canonic Gospel's composition. Others date it to the middle of the 2nd Century, with some believing the Gospel of Thomas is the product of a long educational process with new addendums or developments added to the "original nucleus" until the finished work was concluded towards the middle of the 2nd. Century.

The Discovery of the Nag Hammadi Codexes allowed the identification of the Gospel of Thomas as the "Sayings of Jesus." These were found on Greek papyrus fragments unearthed between 1897 and 1903, near Oxyrhynchus, in lower Egypt, 160 kilometers southwest of Cairo, and dated around 150 A.D.

Among singularities found in the "Gospel according to Thomas," is the fact that despite many similarities with the gospels of the New Testament, "it has its own sources," that is, texts not found in the Synoptic Gospels (Matthew, Mark, and Luke) nor the Gospel according to John. For this reason, several scholars contemplate the possibility that this collection of sayings was initially penned in Greek and dated after the first half of the early first century.

Nature of the Gospel according to Thomas

It has been said that the "Gospel according to Thomas" is a "Gospel of Wisdom."

Even the text itself mentions it in its beginning:

«These are the hidden words that the living Jesus spoke. And Didymus Judas Thomas wrote them down.»

The Coptic term that accompanies the expression "the words" is translated into English as "hidden," although translated into other languages as "secret;" moreover, bringing to mind what the Apostle Paul of Tarsus said in his first epistle to the Corinthians:

> However, we speak wisdom among those who are mature, yet not the wisdom of this age, nor of the rulers of this age, who are coming to nothing. But we speak the wisdom of God in a mystery, the hidden wisdom…
>
> | **1 Corinthians 2:6 & 7a**

Therefore, we can say that the "Gospel according to Thomas" is a "Gospel of Hidden Wisdom," and hidden for the reasons expressed in verse 28: «they are blind in their heart, and they cannot see.»

Therefore, this gospel of early Christianity aspires to impel its readers to "have eyes to see and ears to hear," since the search for God's Kingdom presented by Jesus in this gospel starts with knowing one's own self:

> *When you come to know yourselves, then you will be known, and you will realize that you are*

> *the children of the living Father. But if you do not come to know yourselves, then you exist in poverty, and you are poverty*[73]

| Thomas 3 Apocrypha

| The Gospel of Truth- Valentinus

Not to be confused with Saint Valentine, the saint of lovers or Valentino.

Valentinus, of Egyptian origin and educated in Alexandria, traveled to Rome in the year 135 A.D., along with other renowned church fathers such as Hermas, Marcion, and Justin, to present their writings. In just a short time, he gained a large following due to his substantial knowledge of Christ and the Father, his fame extending beyond Rome.

According to Tertullian,[74] Valentinus was considered a prominent leader to take the position of Bishop of Rome, but his opponent, Irenaeus, completely discredited him.

Irenaeus, with a complete orthodox structure, was radically opposed to any experiences with the Holy Spirit.

This led Irenaeus to embark on a dreadful persecution, discrediting Valentinus and his followers by mixing his teachings with those of the Greek Gnostics in a book called "Against Heresies."

Valentinus called upon the knowledge of the Father through Jesus Christ and the Holy Spirit. In the "Gospel

---

[73] https://www.espiritualidadpamplona-irunea.org/wp-content/uploads/2020/06/-The Gospel of Thomas-.pdf

[74] - One of the prominent fathers of the Church in Northern Africa in the 2nd. Century.

of Truth," he writes about Jesus Christ, who came in the flesh to save humankind. This faith declaration is utterly nonexistent in Gnosticism, which seeks to come to the knowledge of God through the mind. According to this philosophical branch, the world of ideas comes to men through a demiurge that enlightens them.

Irenaeus' triumph resulted in the eradication of spiritual experiences through the Holy Spirit, thereby wholly rejecting the idea that Christ could live within the life of a believer. Clinging to this thought, he engaged on a crusade of burning many 2nd Century writings of great value.

A solid foundation in the Word of God is required to study Valentinus. The great men of God that sought to establish his Light and his kingdom were always controversial, with many of them burned, tormented, and, of course, defamed.

Reading Valentinus in the "Gospel of Truth" was a great blessing to me. But before daring to write anything about him, I carried out in-depth research of his person and many of the early writings.

Unfortunately, much of the information found online is significantly contaminated for those desiring to research him. The most reliable studies can be found at Princeton University as well as at the University of California. These are also translated into Spanish.[75]

By including some of Valentinus's verses in this book, I do not impose anything, but each one is free

---

[75] - The Gnostic Gospels by Elaine Pagels. This book was distinguished in the US with the National Book Critics Circle and the National Book Awards. It has since become the indisputable reference work of the gnostic gospels. In it, Professor Pagels reveals several discrepancies that separated primitive Christians around the very facts of Christ's life, the meaning of His teachings or the form that the His church should have. She describes how gnostic teachings deny the resurrection of Christ and priestly authority. She also describes how orthodox doctrines finally prevailed.

to take it or leave it. However, I found it enormously enlightening and completely analogous to the Bible.

| Lost Books Mentioned In The Bible

|The Book of Jasher

> So, the sun stood still, and the moon stopped, till the nation avenged itself on[a] its enemies, as it is written in the Book of Jasher.
>
> The sun stopped in the middle of the sky and delayed going down about a full day
>
> | Joshua 10:13

> And he told them to teach the children of Judah the Song of the Bow; indeed, it is written in the Book of Jasher. (Another mention of this book made by an important figure, such as the Prophet Samuel, shows that the book of Jasher was quite popular among the Israelitesr.
>
> | 2 Samuel 1:18

| Enoch's Book of Prophecies

> It was also about these men that Enoch, in the seventh generation from Adam, prophesied, saying, "Behold, the Lord came with many thousands of His holy ones,
>
> **| Jude 1:14**

Here, Jude mentions and quotes Enoch's prophecies, highlighting that they were known in that day in time.

LIKE STARS FOR EVERMORE

Like Stars for Evermore
Color Graphics Collection

This special graphics collection contains 14 colorful and enlarged illustrations that are represented in this book, "Like Stars for Evermore" by Ana Méndez Ferrell. This is a great resource to enhance your study of your celestial persona in the Heavenly Places in Christ. Get yours today!

Available on Amazon

Participate in our video course series

www.voiceofthelight.com

If you enjoyed this book, we also recommend

The Spirit of Man

As we understand the origin of where we come from and the image in Whom we were created, we will find our true identity and the power that was given to us. In this book of deep revelation, the author takes us to discover the anatomy of our invisible being. You will learn how we were conceived by God and the different functions of our spirit, soul, and heart. A mystery that has been veiled for centuries, but that God is revealing to us. In this book you will also discover:

- How to reach your highest spiritual potential

- How your Tri-part being functions and interacts in the spiritual and physical dimensions

- The spiritual origin of sickness and health

The Spirit of Man is a true legacy of knowledge that will spiritually develop you in ways you have always longed for.

www.voiceofthelight.com

If you enjoyed this book, we also recommend

Seated In Heavenly Places

This is a book of Reformation that includes the keys to understanding the Government of God and experiencing His power in our lives. This is a work that challenges you to the very core of your being as the Lord takes you to His throne.

These pages, written by Dr. Ana Méndez Ferrell, will allow you to understand the spiritual realm and help you penetrate the most beautiful places and dimensions of the Spirit.

You will be guided on how to see and know God, not when you die, but HERE and NOW.

Get it today

www.voiceofthelight.com

Watch us on **Frequencies of Glory TV** and **YouTube**
Follow us on **Facebook**, **Instagram** and **Twitter**

www.frequenciesofglorytv.com
www.youtube.com/user/VoiceoftheLight

https://m.facebook.com/AnaMendezFerrellPaginaOficial
www.instagram.com/anamendezferrell
www.twitter.com/MendezFerrell

Contact us today!

Voice of The Light Ministries
P.O. Box 3418
Ponte Vedra, FL. 32004
USA
904-834-2447

www.voiceofthelight.com

www.ingramcontent.com/pod-product-compliance
Lightning Source LLC
Chambersburg PA
CBHW060508090426
42735CB00011B/2149